ARCHITECTS' SKETCHES

ARCHITECTS' SKETCHES

DIALOGUE AND DESIGN

KENDRA SCHANK SMITH

AMSTERDAM • BOSTON • HEIDELBERG • LONDON • NEW YORK • OXFORD
PARIS • SAN DIEGO • SAN FRANCISCO • SINGAPORE • SYDNEY • TOKYO
Architectural Press is an imprint of Elsevier

ELSEVIER

Architectural Press

Architectural Press is an imprint of Elsevier
Linacre House, Jordan Hill, Oxford OX2 8DP, UK
30 Corporate Drive, Suite 400, Burlington, MA 01803, USA

First published 2008

British Library Cataloguing-in-Publication Data
A catalogue record for this title is available from the British Library

Library of Congress Cataloging-in-Publication Data
A catalog record for this title is available from the Library of Congress

ISBN: 978-0-7506-8226-8

For information on all Architectural Press publications
visit our website at www.architecturalpress.com

Typeset by Charon Tec Ltd (A Macmillan Company), Chennai, India
www.charontec.com
Printed and bound in Slovenia

08 09 10 11 10 9 8 7 6 5 4 3 2 1

Working together to grow
libraries in developing countries

www.elsevier.com | www.bookaid.org | www.sabre.org

ELSEVIER   BOOK AID
              International   Sabre Foundation

CONTENTS

LIST OF ILLUSTRATIONS

ACKNOWLEDGEMENTS

I would like to thank Stefanie Leontiadis, former graduate assistant at the University of Hartford, for her help with the initial research of images. I would also like to recognize Dmitry Kulikov of the University of Hartford and Erald Kokalari of Ryerson University for their assistance with digital reproduction at various stages of the project. My appreciation goes to Caitlin Bailey who edited much of the text and provided helpful insight.

I would like to thank the University of Hartford for assistance with a research grant and Ryerson University with development funds to help purchase illustrations.

I truly appreciate the generosity of the architects whose sketches are illustrated here. Their assistance, and enthusiasm for the project, was critical to the realization of this book.

I also would like to thank my family, and especially my husband Albert C. Smith, whose support means so much to me.

CHAPTER 1

INTRODUCTION AND THE SKETCH

Figure 1.1 depicts an architect sketching what he observes, which represents one way that architects think with media and use sketches for dialogue. This architect, placed in front of a dynamic and historic construction, may be recording the building's proportions, details, or its placement in context. He may be drawing to try to understand its scale, materiality, or how it compares with

FIGURE 1.1   Triumphal Arch, Tripoli; Plate 4 (engraved by George Harley (1791–1871) 1821 (litho) from *A Narrative of Travels in Northern Africa* by Lyon, Captain George Francis (1795–1832) (after).

other buildings throughout history. He may be trying to replicate how it looks as a way to bring a souvenir home or to preserve its complexities, which may be hard to imprint on his memory without visual stimulus. The architect, possibly on a *Grand Tour*, comprehends more through the action of sketching than mere observation. Forced to study as he imitates, this architect may understand more about the building's construction or intention. Drawing from observation is one dimension of how architects may use sketches as dialogue.

Architects depend upon sketches throughout the process of design as a medium for dialogue. They are the physical manifestation of their thinking and are used in various ways from the inception of the project to final detailing and evaluation. As instruments of a process, they reveal an intimate conversation that is coupled with desire for the future building (Piotrowski and Robinson, 2001). Intention and meaning evident in the use of architectural sketches may be explored by comparing them to theories of play, memory, imagination, and fantasy. A further method of examining the propositions inherent in sketches is to compare them to characteristics of caricature and the grotesque to find less obvious qualities of conscious, or subconscious, intention. Where architects depend upon sketches as the medium for the creative process used to conceive architecture, they also use sketches in all aspects of the design process with individual expression. This examination suggests an interpretation of architects' relationships with the transitory and immediate images they utilize for design.

Because architectural sketches are part of a thinking process and seldom an end product, they play an important role in the process of architectural design. Even though architectural sketches are uniquely personal, there are several general functions which are common to them. Sketches may facilitate discovery and the first inspirations for conceptual beginnings, they can be part of the communication between parties involved in the process, or they are often a means to record mental impressions. Sketches can be employed to evaluate decisions and suggest refinement; they are used as diagrams to analyze a difficult thought, and they help architects to visualize and thus understand complex configurations. As evidenced by cave paintings and images continuously created through history, humans also have an innate desire to represent what they see and what they imagine (Gombrich, 1985).

ARCHITECTURAL SKETCHES AND A COMPARISON TO DIALOGUE

Architects require a visual forum to construe the information necessary for the conception and building of complex structures. This process necessitates a dialogue – a free exchange of thoughts and opinions – between architects and themselves, their clients, the contractors and their colleagues. The discourse implies a two-way interaction, which creates a learning environment, one where the interaction and reasoning facilitates the entire process of design. This dialogue, as a theme throughout this book, implies the fluid and evolving 'give and take' of discussion. It reinforces the thesis, antithesis and synthesis of a design spiral, along with the 'action and reaction' promoting intelligibility (Broadbent, 1973).

With the varied uses of sketches for inspiration and design thinking, communication, recording, evaluation and testing, analysis, visualization and understanding, together with a passion to create images, architects depend upon a representational medium to facilitate the dialogue of these functions. Primarily visual rather than verbal or written, design requires a projection for this conversation. These visual tools help architects communicate with colleagues or engage a personal discussion with their images.

Fraser and Henmi, in their book *Envisioning Architecture*, recognize that drawings, like sketches, have the potential to multiply thought and create a chain of associations that lead to new ways of seeing and understanding. Here it is evident that the acts of visual dialogue enrich the entire process:

> *Just as an author inserts his or her conceptual presence into a drawing through a mode of seeing, interpreting, and changing a scene, drawing tools impose a material influence. Drawing thus intervenes between an author and their ideas being considered, becoming in effect a third presence. In this sense, drawing is not a transparent translation of thought into form, but rather a medium which influences thought just as thought influences drawing. (Fraser & Henmi, 1994: viii)*

Dialogue, according to the *Oxford English Dictionary*, stems from the Greek to 'speak alternately,' and is a verbal interchange or thought between two or more persons. It describes an interaction and implies question and answer. Similar to discourse, it may be accompanied by an act of understanding by which it passes from premises to consequences and includes the faculty of reasoning. This free exchange of thoughts and opinions creates the close acquaintance, or intimacy, of sentiments or observations, opinions and ideas. An intelligibility results from the give and take, and trial and error, profoundly evidenced in the acquisition of knowledge. For architects, when designing, this communication requires a visual component – images that through their power to convince, seduce, compel, argue, and provide insight, fertilize and solidify the infinite number of decisions necessary for a building to be built as it was conceived.

Intention gleaned from images has been demonstrated by the extensive research of iconology and aesthetics. If dialogue, as an analogy for the design process, evokes the relationship between designers themselves and their repertoire of constituents, then sketches become a participant in this acquisition of understanding. Designers engage in conversation on many levels; some of this dialogue is initiated with the intricate questioning and interpretation of a client's needs and desires. In an abstract relationship, designers need to converse with the boundaries of their design, such as codes, site, and functions of the intended outcome. Additional boundaries of dialogue may include the people who support the process such as contractors, consultants, community groups and zoning boards. This conversation includes the issues of design that affect the designers' decisions, such as the history of architecture, current trends or styles, the conceptual strategies imposed on the project, and the designers' whole being (made up of education, sensibilities, experiences, memories, and propensity for imagination).

Architectural drawing, as Edward Robbins writes, has a social dimension. It unites its physical manifestation to the architect, who makes cultural artifacts and acts as a social practitioner (Robbins, 1994). Sketches, by comparison, are in most cases personal notes, references, and analysis. Although used for communication with clients and other people in the building process, much of architects' personal communication in the form of sketches is inherently too vague and unformed to be effective communication to others. When it does occur, this communication may be an ephemeral search for ideas amongst a design team. Beyond the public domain of the drawings being used for communication of construction directives and presentation, sketches represent architects' dialogue, employing a physical manipulation of media in a manifestation of immediate impressions. Directly from the hand, without intermediaries, sketches can be a personal dialogue or a physical remnant of a conversation that depends upon imagery. Thus, the production of a sketch constitutes an action and reaction that provides architects with the interaction necessary to think through the complex process of anticipating a building and nurturing it to final completion.

Dialogue implies the presentation of images, written words or sound used to influence others. How we interpret this stimulus depends on many factors, as visual communication involves perception and interpretation, and is laced with cultural and psychological dimensions. Since any projection of communication in culture depends upon signs, part of this discussion concerns the signifier and that which is signified (Culler, 1986; Buchler, 1955; Eco, 1976; Walker and Chaplin, 1977). Writing on semiotics speculates a relationship between what made the image and the image itself. In contemporary society, the mass communication of media is simultaneously received through different means; we can no longer differentiate and control the media, and thus it becomes omni-present and loses a hierarchy of importance (Kearney, 1988). Society cannot ignore the media's influence, and everything seen and heard is somehow translated, as W.J.T. Mitchell writes, 'this interaction is unavoidable,' and when speaking about 'the innocent eye' he states:

> *When this metaphor becomes literalized, when we try to postulate a foundational experience of 'pure' vision, a merely mechanical process uncontaminated by imagination, purpose, or desire, we invariably discover one of the few maxims on which Gombrich and Nelson agree: 'the innocent eye is blind.' The capacity for a purely physical vision that is supposed to be forever inaccessible to the blind turns out to be itself a kind of blindness. (Mitchell, 1986: 118)*

Comparatively, theorists seek to interpret sketches and, not surprisingly, these sketches confound even the architects who make them. As a way to begin this method of translation, it is important to turn to several philosophers who write about some basic theories of visual communication, intention and interpretation. Once established that all images demand interpretation, it is possible to accept hermeneutics as a method to extrapolate meaning from images. But this meaning may be indeterminate and it is important to recognize, as Saussure states, that '...signs do not refer to objects in any fixed way' (Kearney, 1988: 269; Saussure, 1986). If, as Barthes writes, the authority of the author is diminished, then readers may interpret in any way they please. This opportunity opens interpretation to fragmentation (Barthes, 1988; Kearney, 1988). But by presenting the notion of 'The Third Meaning', the reader, as observer of the image, can find an interpretation beyond simple signs and find an 'obtuse' signifier in the '...power of certain [images] to carry a third level of impact (*significance*) beyond the conventional levels of informational *message* or symbolic *reference*' (Kearney, 1988: 278). Postmodern philosophers write about elusive interpretation and find that in a parodic circle '[t]here is no possibility of a single founding reference' (Kearney, 1988: 252).

With this constant 'mirroring' of reflexivity comes the problem of definitive meaning. The instability opens opportunities for the architect to act as an interpreter and operate between the parts and the whole (Gadamer, 1989). Humans can no longer regulate mass media at the source but, as Eco suggests, concentrate on 'the point of reception' (Kearney, 1988; Eco 1976). 'By affirm-ing the right of each media recipient to give his own meaning to the images and sounds which surround him, are we not in fact leaving the basic system of media consumerism intact?' (Kearney, 1988: 382). This communication might be one-way, but through interpretation or acceptance into our psyche, we are partners in this conversation. This relationship may not be concerned with the definitive interpretation, but instead with utilizing possibilities found through understanding. It is important to recognize the various perspectives viewed in the cultural artifact (Gadamer, 1989). With this inspection the meaning of the 'text' can be extrapolated from its context.

The same may be true of architects' images. They carry potential meaning that can be accepted, rejected, countered, expanded or mutated depending, of course, on the reaction evoked in the human. Sketches and drawings are modes of architectural representation, as they may represent a mental impression of a visual perception of a setting as it is observed. The representation often gives the ability to see beyond appearances to a deeper meaning. The act of drawing facilitates interpreta-tion; this understanding is expressed by Richard Wollheim when he writes 'to see a drawing as a representation of something is no longer to take it, or to be disposed to take it, for that thing: it is rather to understand that thing by it' (Wollheim, 1974: 24). Architects draw to see and subsequently understand, whether it is an observation of perceptual stimulus or from a mental impression con-jured up by imagination. Carlo Scarpa expresses this concept well: 'I want to see things, that's all I really trust. I want to see, and that's why I draw. I can see an image only if I draw it' (Dal Co and Mazzariol, 1984: 242).

Donald Schön writes that much of what defines the 'reflective practitioner' is a designer hav-ing a conversation with the situation. He reinforces the relationship of designers to the way they visualize when he writes '...the graphic world of the sketchpad is the medium of reflection-in-action. ...Because the drawing reveals qualities and relations unimagined beforehand, moves can function as experiments' (Schön, 1983: 157). Schön recognizes how the action of sketching is part of eliciting a certain problem solving activity, and that the translation and application of those images are vital steps in bringing forth a design. 'The act of drawing can be rapid and spontaneous, but the residual traces are stable. The designer can examine them at leisure' (Schön, 1983: 157). As in any conversation, the dialogue with an image is not something that can be predetermined – it is a reaction to each image as it emerges on the page.

Fraser and Henmi suggest that a drawing has two lives: a dialogue with the architect at the time of the actual action of drawing and an afterlife, during which others view and interact with it. 'The influence of drawing then exists independently, acquiring its own voice and its own history through many acts of viewing and interpreting' (Fraser and Henmi, 1994: viii). Architects may be looking for something different each time they sit down to draw, and may discover something other than expected at each sitting. The methods and techniques, although unique to each architect, may also vary depending on the intended outcome and, in a situation of this variety, interpretation may even differ depending upon the time of day or mood of the designer.

A sketch may have many functions and how they communicate to their creator may be vague and allusive. Donald Schön writes about how architects revel in the ambiguous. When drawing, an architect finds himself immersed in '...judgments of quality for which he cannot state adequate criteria, and he displays skills for which he cannot state the rules and procedures. ...It is this entire process of reflection-in-action which is central to the 'art' by which practitioners sometimes deal well with situations of uncertainty, instability, uniqueness, and value conflict' (Schön, 1983: 50).

All images convey something, whether they are ideas, impressions, or emotions, and these communications range from the concrete to the abstract. Bernard Tschumi writes that all architecture represents something – the king, or ideas of God (Tschumi, 1994). These each imply the notion of the signified and the signifier, and of course the interpreters who utilize the information. Conversations are always subject to misinterpretation, inadequacy, implied terms, private jokes, intonation or allusion. They are often too brief, too elaborate, too cryptic, too flowery, too dense, too obtuse, or too pointed in their language, but each event of communication evokes some emotional response, either subtle or overt. Dialogue is woven with the constant interpretation between what has been said and an appropriate response.

Juan Pablo Bonta expresses the indirect learning and added dimension of communication that emerges from an image viewed as an indicator. 'An *indicator* is a directly perceivable event by means of which it is possible to learn something about other events which are not perceivable directly.' The '...queue, ambulance and notice are *indicators* and the occurrence of the accident in their *meaning*' (Bonta, 1979: 26). Each interaction requires a rethinking and a repositioning since dialogue must be a continual interpretation by the human to understand and react, whether actively or passively:

The picture and the actor's fantasy-imaginary are not devices to be borrowed from the real world in order to signify prosaic things which are absent. For the imaginary is much nearer to, and much farther away from, the actual – nearer because it is in my body as a diagram of the life of the actual...farther away from the actual because the painting is an analogue or likeness only according to the body; because it does not present the mind with an occasion to rethink the constitutive relations of things; because, rather...it offers to vision its inward tapestries, the imaginary texture of the real. (Kearney, 1988: 116)

Much dialogue vacillates between the past, present and future: the past that an architect has experienced and the future anticipation of a structure. This adds to the ambiguous nature of the medium and also multiples the effort in the translation.

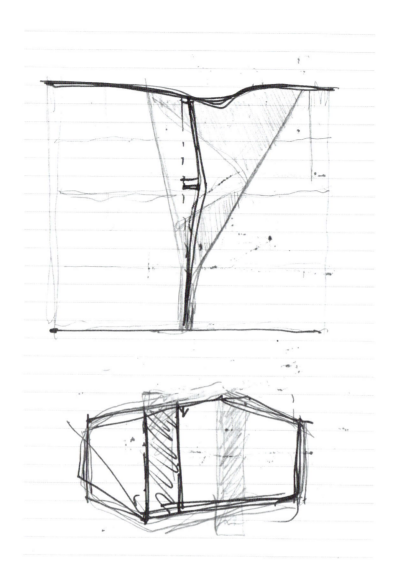

FIGURE 1.2   Lorcan O'Herlihy; Idea sketch of unfolding light well in a structure.

This sketch by Lorcan O'Herlihy (Figure 1.2), although vague and undefined to an observer, speaks of an understanding of materiality and light. O'Herlihy is the founder and principal of the California firm LOHA. His firm began in 1990 with houses utilizing sensitive material juxtapositions. Much of his work plays with light, translucency, transparency, layering, and revealing space. This young firm has been awarded seven American Institute of Architects awards and has been published extensively. Their work includes the housing project Habitat 825, the Palos Verdes Art Center, and Café R&D. On lined notebook paper, this sketch studies an unfolding light well in a structure. With a combination of pencil and ink, it appears the detail was studied first in graphite. O'Herlihy seems to have used faint graphite lines to explore the shape and extension of the wall, and then defined the form with ink. Minimal lines define the entire function of the wall. The way the light well has been folded off the surface of the building presents a complex form and geometry that require perceptive articulation. Architects utilize sketches for many aspects of their design process;

here, the study of a detail reveals the way a sketch assists to envision a three-dimensional form difficult to imagine any other way. O'Herlihy writes about the design process used in the practice:

> *LOHA utilizes various tools such as digital modeling, modeling, and hand sketches in our process. Our work is driven by information and process. Whether it be pencil-to-paper, or computer modeling, these instruments flush out and discover new ideas. Further, analyzing a project through sketches can reveal details that cannot be reflected in a built project; namely, a view into the process of designing.*[1]

Although it provides insight into architects' intention and meaning, this book is a celebration of the ambiguous, undefined, and inspired. The intent is not to look for the definitive or the absolute but to recognize that architects use sketches in various ways, and that these images are entirely too complex to explain completely. Though identifying issues relating to a visual dialogue (memory, imagination, fantasy, play, caricature and the grotesque) helps architects interpret the conversation of imagery that is our discipline, there are seldom definitive meanings evident in sketches; the reward, however, emerges from the unexpected outcomes of the dialogue.

METHODOLOGY

This book constitutes a speculation concerning architectural sketches. It is difficult to generalize about the techniques of the design process since each architect finds his or her own useful approach. This book is less about 'how to' design and more about the evidence of a design process by several diverse architects. It hopes to present some comparisons to help the reader speculate about the role of sketches and how they assist architects. The book is not meant to be definitive but primarily present loose connections that may suggest an intention or meaning. The purpose is to elucidate a complex and undefined process, and through examination view sketches in a new light. In addition, it may be an adoration of sketches' uniqueness when seen as an expression of creativity. The methodology, then, is to attempt to provide insight through comparing architects' sketches to philosophical, artistic, and literary theories. This process is interpretive and hermeneutic. It is not meant to be a codification of specific design methods, but celebrates the diversity of styles, and approaches, from historic and contemporary architects' images.

Many researchers who study architectural sketches have chosen an empirical method to learn about the uses and value of sketches, and this work makes use of their findings. Research has statistically concluded that architects usually begin a design process by asking questions and leaving all options open. These conclusions may be a reinforcement of expected, or logical, suspicions. V. Goel published a study entitled the *Computational Theory of Mind* that specifically explores sketches. His study suggests that '...cognitive processes are computational processes and require a representational medium – *a language of thought* – in which to represent information and to carry out computations' (Goel, 1995: 1). It is fundamental to conclude that architects need a medium to think through design, but to compare sketches to language may give them a symbolic nature suggesting they can be read for specific and definitive meaning. All reading is a matter of interpretation, but associating a specific mark on the paper with a constant and universal meaning is problematic.

Robin Evan wrote that architecture is not language. In his article *Translations from Drawing to Building* Evans speaks about architecture in general but these thoughts could easily extend to drawing. 'All things with conceptual dimension are like language, as all grey things are like elephants. A great deal in architecture may be language-like without being language. Some might say that the recent insistence that architecture is a language is only the last wave of a persistent verbal tide eroding vision, bedeviling our ability to see without language to guide our eyes' (Evans, 1986: 154).

---

[1] When asked to explain how he uses sketches, Lorcan O'Herlihy sent this description.

Likewise, Omer Akin in *Representation and Architecture* contends that design methods are not knowable and teachable:

> *Over the past 15 years there has been an emergence and subsequent regression of 'design method' as a supposed way of going about solving architectural problems or understanding the processes of design... contending that the processes of design are knowable and teachable, these design methods have come to us with a functionalist bias and quasi-scientific aspirations. The assumptions seem to be that if we know the facts, if we order and analyze them correctly, the design solution will follow naturally (and presumably without much interference from the architect). This assumption, that design and its processes can be predicted, is naïve to a fault for if, indeed, the future can be predicted and consequently known before it occurs, then in effect the future becomes part of the present. (Akin and Weinel, 1982: 143)*

By referring to sketches as playful dialogue, it is not intended to imply that sketches are language-like, but rather to solicit the 'give and take' of dialogue that is also experienced in the philosophical ideas of play.

Much insight about the unpredictability of sketches can be extracted from an empirical approach. In most cases, architects have trouble expressing exactly what they are thinking with each line that they draw. In a recent study, Goel equates numerical statistics to the percentage of design development statements that a specific architect makes (Goel, 1995).

Another study by Masaki Suwa, John Gero and Terry Purcell at the University of Sydney questions how a designer is able to 'discover unintended visual/spatial features in sketches' (Suwa et al., 1999: 3). These researchers classify three types of unexpected discoveries. The first type is a unique spatial or organizational relationship never before seen in the process. The second involves the action of reviewing a shape or texture that is essentially a reinterpretation of the original element. The third type is to 'newly perceive an implicit space in-between depictions'.

Their study involved observing an architect in the process of design. They were able to conclude specific percentages of each of these types of actions that happened during the architect's design investigation. They found that, for example, 107 of the unexpected discoveries belonged to the 'relation' type, and the researchers were able to count and codify these statistics (Suwa et al., 1999). Their conclusions may seem logical to architects, when discussing the implications for design education, since they wrote: '[a]n ideal way to cognitively interact with one's own design sketches is to discover as many hidden visual/spatial features in the sketches as possible' (Suwa et al., 1999: 15). Suwa, Gero and Purcell have also concluded that '...when a designer simultaneously pays attention to a set of previously sketched elements which have never been attended to together, he or she is likely to make UXDs [unexpected discoveries]' (Suwa et al., 1999: 17).

In Goel's study, he observes how often architects in his study look to images they have previously been drawing. This fact leads to an important notion that architects utilize memory and visual reference as associative techniques to transform and edit the current images in their focus. Goel also questioned designers' use of symbols and, from his research, confirms several qualities of external symbol systems that most architects use in design:

> *They [external symbol systems] include the facts that (i) designers manipulate representations of the world rather than the world itself, (ii) designers use many different symbol systems, and (iii) different symbol systems are correlated with different problem solving phases and cognitive processes. (Goel, 1995: 127)*

Realizing the limitations of symbol systems is very important to a study of sketches, since a shape may mean something different every time it is drawn. Goel understands this difficulty and writes that 'as we move away from circumscribed puzzle-game domains, like cryptarithmetic, into more open-ended cognitive domains, like planning and design, and continue in the direction of the arts (literature, poetry, painting, music, etc.), cognitive science's ability to explain the relevant cognitive processes approaches zero' (Goel, 1995: 6).

Zafer Bilda and John S. Gero performed a small study using three architects as subjects. They recorded verbalized segments inspecting these designers' intentions (Bilda and Gero, 2005). These segments consisted of thoughts about an aspect of a current image of interest. They compared these interactions when the architect sketched blindfolded and when allowed to see. Bilda and Gero concluded that architects are more productive when using imagery in contrast to relying totally on memory. 'From the first 20 minutes of the session to the remaining time in the sessions, the overall cognitive activity in blindfolded condition each time dropped below the overall cognitive activity in sketching condition' (Bilda and Gero, 2005: 158). This study reminds architects that sketches work to spark memories and associative thoughts. Designers might sketch an image and, once it is comprehended, they can immediately react with another image in a conversation with the pencil and paper. There is much research using this methodology that informs the design process for architects and, although this empirical research is incredibly valuable, this book revels in the inconsistency of architects' forms and depends primarily on association and speculation to conclude intention.

The graphic images of sketches are two-dimensional, three-dimensional, and often digital, visual collections of marks which can be manipulated. Since they are easily transformable images, they play a major role in architectural thinking. They allow architects to transform and re-form them to influence conceptual discovery and refinement. The manipulation of the sketch affects the understanding of architecture, and this comprehension requires reflection and interpretation. Sketches are the translation of the character or appearance of a concept into an understandable or useable form. This often constitutes the transformation of a physical object or concept into another dimension or medium. Comparing the representational qualities of sketches to definitions of memory, imagination, fantasy, play, and traditional uses of caricature and the grotesque discloses the tangible and intangible aspects which make them fundamental in any process of design.

It is through exploring memory, imagination, fantasy, and play that the faculties of the mind can be realized in these images. Using research into the nature of memory, imagination and fantasy assists a discussion of how these elements can be viewed in sketches. The study of play, in the philosophical sense, reveals similar methods of manipulation as practiced by architects. This study proposes to find ways in which architectural sketches' likeness to elements of caricature and the grotesque offer important keys to their uses and how they are understood.

Sketches, caricature and the grotesque all depend upon a certain amount of resemblance. The similarity is often a matter of interpretation involving likeness to a referent. The transformative aspects of caricature and the grotesque in their simplicity, deformation, condensation, transformation, and exaggeration project a poignant view, as does a sketch. This book questions how the intermediary qualities of the known and the unknown in the grotesque echo the ambivalent and transitory quickness of a graphic image. It will also raise issues of ridicule in caricature and paradox in the grotesque, to explore their importance for sketching in architecture.

The implicit challenge is to raise issues of architectural sketches as representation and comprehend their complex positions within architecture. This discussion may also extend to how a study of architectural sketches can influence or replicate a conception of architecture. Does the way we draw, and more importantly our movement to digital methods, affect the completed construction? Wolfgang Meisenheimer states this proposition well: 'and the question arises of whether a new, different understanding of architectural *drawing* alludes to a new and different understanding of *architecture*!?' (Meisenheimer, 1987: 119).

This question is extremely difficult for a book to examine because it encompasses all of architecture. In an attempt to limit its scope, this investigation will touch on the interpretation of architectural conception through the examination of architectural sketches. Probing these images should reveal some of their conversational characteristics and the dependence of the design process on sketches.

This book explores the visual qualities of sketches; it is the observation of marks on a page. These marks indicate something to the architects who make them and, consequently, studying the remnants from the process should present insight into their uses. The sketch is an image that comprises a collection of forms standing for an object or thought as a representation, not necessarily including a program or statement of intention. James Smith Pierce suggests the problem of intent when examining drawings from history:

> *If he [the architect] has not set down his purpose in writing and his age has left no substantial body of theoretical writing or criticism to help us gauge his intent, we must follow the traces of his hand preserved in those drawings that are records of his mind and spirit. (Pierce, 1967: 59)*

Few architects are able to communicate verbally their thoughts during the design process, although they may write about their theories and philosophies pertaining to concepts or precedent in their architecture. By concentrating on the traces of the hand, this study discusses issues that look to what can be observed in the physical sketch and finds comparisons to historical theories of representation. Like an archeologist, this study tries to isolate forms and techniques that suggest a method of design. It is hoped that the comparison to philosophical and literary principles will clarify the 'mind and spirit' as seen in the physical tracings.

However, finding importance in the image as a two-dimensional form is not the same as locating symbolic meaning. While these sketches can be attractive, their beauty is not part of the equation. Their thinking, discovering, evaluating, recording, visualizing, communicating and interpreting abilities stem from their relationship to the architect's design activity. Louis I. Kahn discusses this relationship with reference to the sculptor, Rodin, when he writes how artists can sketch while still envisioning the three-dimensional form:

> *The drawings this great sculptor [Rodin] made took form with his eye on the final results in stone. Although working with seemingly sloppy washes and careless lines, he was always thinking in terms of his chisel and hammer. They are great drawings because they embody the hidden potentialities of his medium. They are the true visions of a creator. A biographer of Rodin explained that his drawing betrayed the divine impatience of the artist who fears that a fleeting impression may escape him: (Kahn, 1991: 11).*

The impetus for this book grew out of many years of observing sketches. After a period of time, certain themes began to emerge. In an obvious way, memory, imagination and fantasy were clearly qualities of sketches, since these three faculties of the mind are tied to creativity and image-making. The playful characteristics exhibited by sketches followed the realization that many architects sketch with great abandon and most see little value in the physical object of the sketch once they have served the process of design.

A definition of play as being representative, having boundaries to stretch against, involving 'give and take' and the immersion in a captivating creative activity are qualities that can be compared to sketches in a design process. The way in which architects manipulate and exaggerate led to research into caricature and the grotesque. Exposing a new 'truth' from deformation is a crucial issue in the distinctly visual aspects of sketches which may be compared to caricature and the grotesque.

After identifying these general topics sketches were chosen for their ability to reveal these themes for discussion; those that implied dialogue in particular were embraced. Sketches were then solicited from architects who generously allowed their reproduction.

This investigation will discuss architectural sketches using two basic approaches. Chapters 2 and 3 take properties inherent in sketches and, as a form of demarcation, reveal their contingency on memory, imagination, fantasy and play. The two chapters discuss aspects which comprise sketches as mental faculties. These faculties of the mind assist in understanding architectural sketches.

Chapters 4 and 5 discuss caricature and the grotesque, illuminating aspects of architectural sketches by comparison to established concepts of both image and likeness transformation. Caricature and the grotesque have historic meaning in literature and art as a process by which to reveal a truth. This study will, among other things, help to discover how architects use sketches, reveal how drawing affects the way they think, show architects' play with a drawing medium and paper, and expose some of the characteristics of architectural sketches.

The concluding chapter discusses the issues which tie this all together – *likeness*, the sketch's characteristics, and the importance of sketches for the entire design process. The last chapter will also explore experiments with digital media as a further exploration of sketches. As a basis and introduction for the chapters, it is necessary to discuss the boundary circumscribing the concept of architectural sketches in relationship to drawing.

Thus, the methodology of this study is less concerned with empirical study and instead relies on observation, comparison, analogy, metaphor, and speculation to rejoice in a creative process.

THE NATURE OF SKETCHES

The 'look' of a sketch is not as important as the role it plays in the design process. Architects have at some times used sketches extensively and, in other periods, employed different modes of representation. Greek architects designed using words and precedent, and consequently sketches are not mentioned. Details were described by the use of *Paradeigma* (Coulton, 1977: 55–58). Medieval builders used full-scale templates and models but relied mostly on plans. Renaissance architects used section perspective drawings along with plans and elevations. Many sketches by Alberti, Michelangelo, and Leonardo are preserved and reflect their interest in orthographic projections. Likewise, students of the *Ecole des Beaux Arts* used plan, section and elevation. When conceiving a project they produced a drawing called an *Equisse* (Hewitt, 1985: 2).

Modern architects clearly use sketches to a great degree. Le Corbusier, for example, sketched in many notebooks and referred back to them often (Le Corbusier, 1981). Architects today use sketches extensively, even to publish and exhibit their conceptual images, and architects such as Frank Gehry and Aldo Rossi have exceptionally thoughtful sketches (Smith, 2005).

The drawing in architecture is a look to the past, present and the future as much as it is a mode for understanding. Filarete, the Renaissance architect, writes that drawings are extremely valuable in representing what a building will be:

It is impossible to explain clearly this business of building if it is not seen in a drawing. It is even difficult to understand it in a drawing. Anyone who does not understand drawing cannot understand it well, for it is more difficult to understand a drawing than it is to draw…For this [reason] let no one value drawing lightly. There is nothing made by the hand that does not partake of drawing in one way or another. Anyone who wishes to know it as it should be [known] can only do it by great exertion of the intellect. (Filarete, 1965: 70)

Drawing is a general term, whereas sketching is a specific technique within the category of drawing. Both can take the form of action or object, verb or noun, as they each imply movement. These words can also be analogies for other actions not involving a specific mark on paper. 'To draw on', 'to draw it up' and 'back to the drawing board' are phrases in the vernacular that do not necessarily mean actual rendering. A quick skit by a comedian is deemed a 'sketch' although it does not involve the mark of a pencil. A dictionary's definitions of 'draw' reveal some intriguing concepts:

Draw – 1. 6. 16. To cause to come, move, or go (from or to someplace, position or condition); to lead, bring, take, convey, put…42. To cause a flow of (blood, matter, 'humors') to a particular part…48. To deduce, infer…59. 66. To make a demand or draft upon (a person, his memory, imagination, etc…) for resources or supplies of any kind. (Oxford English Dictionary)

This definition allows a comprehensive dimension of the word *draw* and provides the ability to see meanings inherent in the word. Often, looking to definitions provides a new interpretation by which unusual connotations may appear. For example, the first definition of *draw* refers to action: to cause (anything) to move toward oneself by the application of force or to pull. The implication is that drawing is an intentional action, a movement towards a goal. The next definition – to contract, cause to shrink; to pull out of shape or out of place, to distort – emphasizes the notion of distortion that evokes the exaggeration and transformation of caricature and the grotesque.

Action also figures in the definition 'to cause to come' or 'to lead'; the 'leading' sense of the word *draw* has connotations for architecture. Drawing may lead to architecture, or the architect can 'lead' the building through drawing. The movement of the line can also 'lead' the architect's eye and thus the mind. Another definition expresses the meaning of draw as 'to cause to flow'. This may be echoed in the beginning sketches of an architectural design process. The quick sketches and analogies, and the coordination of eye, hand, and brain are the thought processes which may encourage architecture 'to flow' forth.

The ability of drawings to help architects 'deduce or infer' is also distinctive of their capacity to assist in making design conclusions. A later definition suggests the drawing's capability to act as architectural representation because the drawing makes a demand upon a person's memory or mental image-making capacities. To draw on resources compels the 'drawing' to pull out the assets of the architect.

A more obscure definition – to trace (a line or figure) by drawing a pencil, pen, or the like, across a surface; to cut (a furrow) by drawing a ploughshare through the soil, and to determine or define the limit between two things or groups – suggests 'draw' as the movement across a surface where the connotation of the object (as the line) is implied. Subsequently, the drawing of a ploughshare through the soil might suggest that the scar on the land is a drawing. This large-scale drawing allows a fresh consideration of what a drawing is, its techniques and media. This is reminiscent of Alberti's use of the word *Lineamenta*, which translated by Joseph Rykwert means 'lines', or 'linear characteristics' (Alberti, 1988: 7, 422–423). This 'trough line' has linear characteristics and questions how a line can be a demarcation. It is possible to wonder whether a three-dimensional ditch can be a line and how theories of representation might translate such a concept.

Authors writing about art and basic design stress that drawing involves line. At the most basic level David Lauer describes a line as 'a mark made by a pointed tool' (Lauer, 1979: 151). Drawing involves making marks with a pointed tool, and those marks are initiated by movement and a force. In reverse, eyes follow a line, and with that action the 'line's potential to suggest motion is basic' (Lauer, 1979: 151). A line or mark made with the bodily action of hands has the ability to cause reflective action as it attracts the human eye to follow it. This cognitive action spurs new associative thoughts, as the line evokes emotional associations (Lauer, 1979).

Filarete writes about what mathematicians knew in the Renaissance: that a line consisted of dots placed consecutively in space (Filarete, 1965). The connection of dots marks time, as do the associative and active qualities of line, so that line and also drawing itself evoke allusions to memory. This seems especially possible when thinking of one aspect of the word *line*: that of lineage. The motion of line and drawings leads to a form of drawing which is the sketch.

According to the *Oxford English Dictionary*, a sketch is a brief description or outline 'to give the essential facts or points of, without going into details'. It can also be a two-dimensional or three-dimensional action documenting primary features of something or 'as preliminary or preparatory to further development'. For the sake of this book it will be assumed that the word *sketch* means a two-dimensional mark. The sketches may or may not be quick in terms of time, or necessarily lacking in detail. The sketch for an architect may be a mode to discover a concept at the beginning of a project, but it can be used in all stages of the design process and even as an observational recording long after the building is constructed. Werner Oechslin writes about a historical definition of the sketch:

In 1681, Baldinucci wrote in his Vocabulario Toscano dell 'Arte del Disegno:
'Sketch /sketches: what the painters call those extremely light strokes of the brush or pencil which they use to outline their concepts without elaborating them to any greater detail; that is what they call

sketching'...the Italians call them Squizzi, from squizzare, meaning to run out and pour out forcefully. (Oechslin, 1982, 101–103)

'To run out' suggests motion, a distinctive quality of sketches. Certainly 'to run out' and 'pour out forcefully' suggest the sketch's speed, but it is not necessary that the sketch be completed quickly. 'Quickness' is inherent in a sketch, but the quickness is not only a matter of time.

Much of the 'motion' of a sketch comes from the physical action of the body. Holding 'the pointed tool' and making it move is vital to an aspect of drawing. In touching the drawing, the tool becomes an extension of the body and reflects the human body. The psychologist and philosopher James Gibson writes about human contact with a drawing: 'the movement of the tool over the surface is both felt and seen' (Gibson, 1979: 275). The 'gesture' of this intimate participation with a sketch gives it meaning and individuality. The control of hand on drawing tool yields not a consistent line but one that is varied, thick or thin. It is this gesture which may provide a case against the use of computers as a replacement for hand sketches. In many stages of design the quality of the mark is important, since individual line produces association in the architect's mind.

Gesture is a body movement that expresses or symbolizes a thought; this body motion can be extended to sketches through the hand. Gesture is also a technique of drawing in fine art, which is to sketch quickly to illustrate the mass and position of a figure. To add another dimension to 'gesture', along with 'gestation' it has the same etymological root which according to the *Oxford English Dictionary* means to bear, carry or act. As with drawing, sketching depends upon movement, and inherent in this movement is visual perception.

This expressive sketch by Steven Holl (Figure 1.3) illustrates thoughtful use of a sketchbook. Steven Holl and Associates is a New York City based firm doing projects such as the Nelson Atkins Museum of Art in Kansas City Missouri, the Museum of Contemporary Art in Helsinki and Simmons Hall, residential housing at the Massachusetts Institute of Technology in Cambridge, Massachusetts. Having been honored with numerous American Institute of Architects Honor Awards, Holl's architecture is concerned with the ethereal and textural qualities of cladding. Surface acts as skin as it is luminous or modeled. The pair of sketches for a pair of 'live work lofts' face each other in a sketchbook. Here, Holl could reference the plan and the three-dimensional form at the same time.

The left side shows a plan that has been annotated with instructions concerning materials, dimensions, and structure. This sketch contains visual notes for decision-making. In the center of the sketch is a service core for the building, showing organization and circulation. The exterior

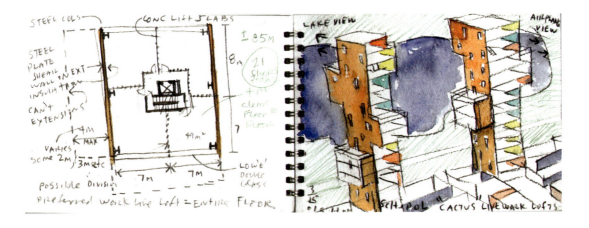

FIGURE 1.3   Steven Holl; Cactus Towers, Live Work Lofts.

walls show *poché* thickness and reveal reminders about materials such as 'steel plate' and 'insulation'. The sketch provides definitive information concerning dimension and steel columns, but it also conveys uncertainty. A note on the bottom left corner explains 'possible division' and to complement this thought visually, the interior walls have been drawn with dotted lines. The dotted lines may have been drawn perforated to express their temporality or to question the decision as to where to place them.

The colorful sketch to the right is less concerned with materiality, instead showing the walls one line thick. Whether intentionally designing the towers to resemble cacti with jutting floors, or realizing the likeness later, Holl has created a playful cartoon-like expression of the lofts. He did not need to present a precise or detailed rendering because the impression was clear from his brief sketch. Using watercolor, he was able to easily differentiate floors and walls to make the image appear three-dimensional, showing interior as well as exterior space. The imprecise edges add texture and energy to the sketch. Notes on the sketch on the right help to remember views while illustrating the lake. Holl's use of media suggests a sense of time as he worked between the two drawings. The ground has been rendered with a green medium, and additional wording shows on the left with the same green. It is possible that after he viewed the size and proportions of the towers, he then added the note to the plan: '21 floors total'.

VISUAL PERCEPTION AS IT PERTAINS TO ARCHITECTURAL SKETCHES

It is important, at this point, to discuss bodies and the occurrence of visual perception. An analysis of visual perception elucidates how architectural sketches are viewed and possibly how they are comprehended. Many psychologists support a well-known theory that the portrayal which appears upside-down on the human retina is like a picture, specifically, Rudolph Arnheim (1969). From his studies, however, James J. Gibson has disputed this theory. Gibson believes '...a retinal image is not something to be looked at by an observer. It is, therefore, profoundly unlike a picture. There is a distribution of energy on a sensory mosaic, but it is not like a replica, or a copy, or a model, or a record' (Gibson, 1982: 261). Gibson is looking at visual perception in an unusual way, because he writes that the light and colors seen do not immediately record themselves in the eye. The brain must perform an interpretation and translation of the 'mosaic' seen. Gibson strengthens his argument by referring to the structure of the eyes of an insect, explaining that they 'see,' but they do not have the capacity in their multi-segmented eyes to perceive a meaningful depiction. They do perceive shapes, colors, movement, and especially light, which can be deciphered for use (Gibson, 1982: 261).

Arnheim's and Gibson's positions may not be as opposed as this implies. Gibson seems to be writing from an interpretive hermeneutic approach, where Arnheim presents an objectivist argument. The largest question might be the word *image* and how much interpretation must be made to understand this array of light and colors as a mental impression. 'Mental impressions' implies 'vision with meaning' rather than passive imagination. It is particularly compelling to agree with Gibson since he suggests the importance of interpretation.

James Gibson implies that it is possible to see form, shapes and color revealed by light, but that it is the brain that translates these perceptions into mental impressions (Gibson, 1982). It could be possible then that a drawn illusion does not allow for the interpretive activity of the imagination. On the other hand, an abstract allusion may allow the brain to interpret, and architects or designers may receive mental impressions from these esoteric beginnings. Sketches, regardless of their degree of ambiguity, have meaning as form generators. This action is reminiscent of the childhood game of finding objects in the abstraction of floating clouds. It is also similar to Leonardo da Vinci's finding of cognitive associations in the stains on rocks (Summers, 1981).

Allusion in ambiguity will be discussed at great length with the associative qualities of imagination in Chapter 3. To add to this line of reasoning, Gibson finds that a '...picture cannot at the same time possess high fidelity for something concrete and high univocality for something abstract' (Gibson, 1982: 248). Richard Wollheim supports this theory and writes '...whereas we cannot, at one and the same moment, see a picture as a configuration and as *trompe l'oeil*' (Wollheim, 1974: 29). It is not possible to mistake a two-dimensional picture for the visual perception of our three-dimensional surroundings when the mind is thinking of it as a flat illusion. Although it is conceivable that the descriptive illusion is more informative, the indefinite image may prove more richly suggestive. Gibson's former students, in their selected collection of essays, discuss perception as seen by their teacher. They also introduce an important aspect of this study: caricature.

> He [Gibson] hypothesized that a faithful picture is a surface that reflects a sheaf of light rays to a point that is the same as the sheaf of rays coming from the depicted scene. According to this view a picture performs its representational function by providing the eye with the same variations in light energy as would the depicted scene...Thus, a line drawing, which preserves relational information but not a point-by-point projection of light energies, may provide as accurate information as a photograph...Caricatures are paradoxical in that they do not present either the same sheaf of rays or the same nested visual solid angles as the things they represent; yet, in a sense they are more faithful representation than photographs. (Gibson, 1982: 226–227)

The caricature, as a way to view a sketch, can present an added dimension to the original. Its likeness to the original is selective, rather than being dependent upon a 'faithful picture'. The selective emphasis of artwork exaggerates or clarifies what the observer sees, and thus accentuates an understanding (Gibson, 1982). Gibson's discussion is valuable for architectural sketches because it proposes an important question: since perception has little resemblance to an image (two-dimensional combination of marks), does drawing an illusion promote understanding?

This is a thought-provoking question that can begin an exploration of the cognitive act of seeing. The sketch can portray an important mode of comprehension, as Maurice Merleau-Ponty expresses when discussing Klee and Matisse: 'the line no longer imitates the visible; it "renders visible"; it is the blueprint of a genesis of things' (Merleau-Ponty, 1964, 183). 'Rendering visible' implies an understanding deeper than an illusion. This may be a distinct feature of sketches, which are often incomplete and vague. Again, this is reminiscent of the sketch's role in 'seeing' as understanding. The architect's mind must be able to immerse itself in the making (Gibson, 1982). In a similar way, Louis I. Kahn writes about seeing and expresses this relationship to understanding:

> There is no value in trying to imitate exactly. Photographs will serve you best of all, if that is your aim. We should not imitate when our intention is to create – to improvise...The capacity to see comes from persistently analyzing our reactions to what we look at, and their significance as far as we are concerned. The more one looks, the more one will come to see. (Kahn, 1991: 11)

An architect must visualize within the confines of a substitute medium to project him- or herself within the frame and flatness of two dimensions. Much of our knowledge is acquired through pictures, and Gibson acknowledges this second-hand learning. 'The learner must ordinarily be given acquaintance with objects, places and events which he has never physically encountered' (Gibson, 1982: 242). This is especially important to architects, as they are dealing with future buildings. A sketch provides a substitute for the object with which to project possible solutions. Learning may emerge from manipulating a substitute, or acquaintance with the future through a sketch.

This beautifully atmospheric sketch of the Staglieno Cemetery in Genoa by Antoine Predock (Figure 1.4) conveys an observed scene and also requires interpretation. Antoine Predock is an architect known for his remarkable architecture integrated with the landscape of the southwestern

FIGURE 1.4　Antoine Predock; Staglieno Cemetery, Genova, Italy, 1988.

United States. He is the 2006 American Institute of Architects Gold Medal recipient and has completed projects such as the Spencer Theater for the Performing Arts in New Mexico in 2004. Based in Albuquerque, New Mexico, his practice found prominence responding to the unique desert environment, repeating forms and colors of the landscape, and focusing intense desert light. More recent projects include the US Federal Courthouse in El Paso, Texas, and the National Palace Museum in Taiwan.

Rendered with a soft medium such as chalk or pastel crayons, the cemetery follows the slope of a hillside. The grave stones appear to emerge out of a mist as their tops are articulated with ink, while the lower portions disappear into what seems to be foliage. The central figure is indistinct in scale as it could be as large as a church or as small as a mausoleum. When asked to comment about the sketch, Predock describes the shift in scale: '[a]t a distance, a city with an amazing miniaturizing shift of scale at close range'. The road in the foreground has been defined by only a few lines but sets the stage for the stones. This sketch is compelling, as figures seem to come forward and recede when the observer focuses on them. A mosaic of colors, depth, and dimension appear out of the dark and light tones. The soft indistinct technique provokes an atmosphere of overgrown decay. Some of the forms suggest human figures. It seems Predock did not need to bring a realistic view home with him; the hazy scene creates an impression of the experience and also elicits interpretation.

In the making of a drawing or painting, the messages evident in the artwork reinforce perceptual stimulation. The artist or architect perceives a line and responds with another. Gibson believes it is reasonable to suppose that humans can think in terms of drawings (Gibson, 1982). Conversely, but consistent with his theories of visual perception, there cannot be vision without the cognitive action of thought.

As a definition of sketches implies, they are often notoriously imprecise, valueless physically, and seen as a means to find something, or communicate, rather than as prized objects in and of themselves. They are usually, but not necessarily, loose, and lacking in detail. Frank Lloyd Wright claimed to have often progressed directly to a stage of drawing up a building without using any conceptual sketches (Hewitt, 1985). On the contrary, other architects may make simple but precise diagrams. Still others may use sketches purely for communication with other architects or the client. Whatever technical method an architect uses, they all touch, if ever so briefly, on a period of conception where the design is in beginning stages, and thus in dialogue they consist of tentative and incomplete thoughts.

The medium (pencil, paper, clay, charcoal or computer) is not important when defining sketches; how they perform for design intention renders their value. Sketches may be three-dimensional in that assembling sticks, planes or volumes also allows an immediate view. Architects may use a soft medium to blur lines and make the drawing expressive yet vague enough to elicit association. Some architects use inexpensive tracing paper, while others choose a more formal medium. Some diagram in the fashion of the *parti* and others carefully redraw a known building to caricature it in a method of deformation and transformation. Computers conjure images that are quickly manipulated and can be either precise or imprecise. Such varied media make establishing a definition of sketches more difficult. When used by different architects, specific media techniques may appear substantially unalike.

In an attempt to identify what sketches are, this study proposes that sketches acquire many physical shapes, but that their similarities lies in how and why architects use them. Since it has been suggested that they are outlines or essential points, often as 'preparations for further development', it seems necessary to differentiate and further describe them as being illustrative of both the design process and their function for the architect. For example, Filarete cleverly uses the analogy of the building as a human body to explain the design process (Filarete, 1965). He writes about the stages of design as being comparable to conception, gestation, birth and nursing.

Stemming from their relationship to function, it is necessary to expand the description of architectural sketches and treat them as illustrative of their use in the design process. Architects often employ sketches for conceptual design to discover or attain knowledge, to accompany brainstorming, and to find allusions or associations. Architects also use sketches to communicate with both colleagues and themselves. The sketch becomes the medium that communicates concepts to others in an office and also helps express emotional or poetic concepts. Architectural sketches can be applied to facilitate communication with, or to impress, a client. These examples make clear that the sketch plays a communicative role beyond that of a mere messenger.

Architects also use sketches to record; they can be used to record a likeness or a fleeting impression. They may be a travel companion to aid visual recollection or to register an emotion or a thought. In another way, architects often employ sketches to visually test abstract conceptual forms. They may be used to 'try something out for fit,' as a type of evaluation. Similarly, the sketch could help to conclude the formation of a mental image.

This sketch of the 'Black Diamond' by Morten Schmidt (Figure 1.5) of schmidt hammer lassen poignantly presents the essence of the Royal Library Extension in Copenhagen, Denmark. The architectural firm of schmidt hammer lassen is a successful and innovative practice based in Århus,

FIGURE 1.5   Morten Schmidt; Extension of the Royal Danish Library, Copenhagen.

Denmark, with offices in Copenhagen, London, and Oslo. Using steel and glass to create luminous boxes they have won numerous awards for their work. A few of their more recent projects include the Royal Library in Copenhagen, residence halls and educational facilities for Kolding Technical College in Kolding, Denmark, the Aalborg Airport, Denmark, and a Culture Center in Nuuk, Greenland.

Everything in this sketch is secondary to the large dark parallelogram of the library extension. The dramatic view shows distinctly the presence of the building on the waterfront in Copenhagen. The background and foreground are lighter and less defined. The buildings in the distance are rendered with quick vague lines. The pedestrians in the foreground are brief profiles. Schmidt emphasizes the bold slice through the building contrasting its lighter value and adding to its transparency. Simplifying the dark shape into a bold form anticipates the final construction but also acts conceptually to identify the building's stark shape – thus the 'Black Diamond'.

The windows on the lower level have been shown as quick 'n' and 'm' shapes in contrast to the amount of time to darken the façade. With the layering of tones, it is possible to view the horizontal levels of the floor through the graphite lines. This has an ability to replicate the final effect of the glass curtain wall. Although a freehand sketch, Schmidt has employed a straight edge to render the bricks on the adjacent building and achieve other straight lines such as the balconies. This combination of ruled and sketchy lines adds to the dynamic expression of the image. As preliminary and preparatory, this sketch uses various techniques to explain more about the building to the architect.

HOW ARCHITECTS USE SKETCHES

It seems crucial at this point to emphasize the way in which architects utilize sketches. This study proposes that architects employ sketches in many stages of the design process. These uses may fall into several areas that could be grouped as discovery, communication, visualization, recording and evaluation. These groupings may be typical, but not necessarily all-inclusive, as each individual architect manipulates sketches in his or her own unique way. The following chapters will discuss these uses of architectural sketches in greater depth, but it is necessary to introduce and outline them as a basis for beginning.

Most architects use the first sketch to visualize and discover early concepts. These sketches in the design process are first impressions. Gerd Neumann, when asked about first sketches, wrote about their purpose for design: 'first sketches which in the form of first conceptual notes are the first step in every realistic design process that is determined by a given task' (Hölzinger *et al*, 1982: 55). An early design sketch often sparks the architect's mind to produce mental impressions and may take on the role of being visual assistance to brainstorming. The architect's imagination is open to many possibilities, as in a beginning stage no potentiality is ruled out. These options might be fragmented and vague, but they originate a thinking process, since this first sketch often must be drawn with great speed to capture the rapid flashes of mental stimulation.

Werner Oechslin feels the sketch is the appropriate medium for designing 'the sketch is ideally suited for capturing the fleetingness of an idea' (Oechslin, 1982: 103). If the sketch itself is a brief outline then it may, in fact, reflect the swift thoughts in the mind. With an analogy to literature, Roderich Fuess treats the sketch as more than an architect's tool: '[f]or Joyce the first sketch is not the initiation into the process of writing, it is much more comparable to pinning down an almost invisible butterfly with an unsteady stylus' (Fuess, 1982: 26). This quote emphasizes the intangible qualities of a sketch. Architects may begin to draw early impressions that could lead to associative impulses, making the whole process difficult to circumscribe. The mental reflection of imagination is not always an escape to the illusionary; it can also be a pondering of associations to attain new knowledge. Italo Calvino looks at one aspect of imagination involving possibilities and association:

> *Still there is another definition in which I recognize myself fully, and that is the imagination as a repertory of what is potential, what is hypothetical, of what does not exist and has never existed, and perhaps will never exist but might have existed…The poet's mind, and at a few decisive moments the mind of the scientist, works according to a process of association of images that is the quickest way to link and to choose between the infinite forms of the possible and the impossible. The imagination is a kind of electronic machine that takes account of all possible combinations and chooses the ones that are appropriate to a particular purpose, or are simply the most interesting, pleasing, or amusing. (Calvino, 1988: 91)*

It is interesting that in his book *Six Memos for the Next Millennium*, Calvino discusses imagination in a chapter he titles 'Visibility'. In the imagination, the combinations and possibilities can first come to light, and they become visible through association. Architect's sketches can act as allusions and these connections might provide new information in a mode of discovery. This first category of the manner in which architects employ sketches leads to another: communication.

Sketches are a medium architects employ to communicate both with colleagues and with themselves. These messages may be facts, emotions, expressions or concepts, depending upon the specific purpose. Since most architects rarely work alone and there are many people with whom they must interact, the sketch often becomes an emissary for information. The completion of a building hinges on the close interaction between the design team and their consultants, most prominent of course being the client. Architects speak to each other through sketches, expressing concepts and advancing their views with visual support. A design architect may converse with his or her team utilizing rough sketches as preparatory for more complex plans, elevations, and sections. Architects, often more visual than verbal, may prefer to communicate with images rather than words.

Communication with the client involves information exchange, but it also implies something more. The position of the architect as a manipulator of images (depiction of form either mental or dimensional) can impress the client with an ability to create an illusion on paper. This skill, regarded with awe by the layman, gives the architect a position of respect. The status is significant in the relationship between the architect and client.

The communicative dialogue of sketches is also vital to the architect for the individual thought process. The sketches may contain emotions, expressions and allusions, as they are poetic drawings, which try to depict the indefinable. They are described by Wolfgang Meisenheimer in terms of '…traces of the memory and the dreams of the drawer, outbreaks of temperament and wit, provocations of the observer, riddles, vague evocations or gestures of philosophical thesis…The transferals and interpretations which result from them move on all possible levels' (Meisenheimer, 1987: 111).

The individual dialogue requires mental and associative reflections that are not necessarily distinct from each other. In a broad sense, architects interviewed concerning their first sketches in the 1987 issue of *Daidalos* see them as agents for discovery and manipulation:

> *Sketches are blinks of the eye, snapshots of the creative process. They are resting points for the wandering intellect on the quest for form – needed for keeping track and for checking; for being able to go back and find a new linear approach to an entangled train of thought, or even to take up an altogether different course.*
>
> *Sketches are catalysts for the mind and, at the same time, the basis for return.*
>
> *Sketches are, to all intents and purposes, the medium of change. They represent a manifestation of the various stages of the process of 'taking shape', of the quest for the ultimate form. (Meisenheimer, 1987: 37)*

Poetic sketches may be distinctly personal, but they perform a function that allows architects to view abstract possibilities. The knowledge that sketches translate to something else gives them meaning for architects. Poetic (not intended to imply without structure) employs allusion and metaphor to describe less tangible things. Richard Wollheim expresses the significance of the dialogue between architects and this ambiguous medium, and touches on an expanded issue of representation. 'Now my suggestion is that in so far as we see a drawing as a representation, instead of as a configuration of lines and strokes, the incongruity between what we draw and what we see disappears' (Wollheim, 1974: 22).

Since the media and technique of a sketch may have extensive consequences for communication, it is necessary to touch briefly on intention. What architects propose to say affects the choice of media and technique, and consequently what they hope to gain from the sketch. This returns to the notion of a poetic sketch, because an abstract technique of drawing provides an ambiguous result, which may either allow for the viewer's own interpretation or permit the architect's associative powers to prevail. For example, the use of ink and wash produces an extremely different result than a number two pencil does. Similarly, the choice of a 'type' of drawing affects the way an idea is interpreted. As an example, Andreas Reidemeister writes about the divergent purpose of a perspective in comparison to that of a sketch. '[S]ketch and perspective view have been opposite poles: the perspective view directed at appearances and persuasion, the sketch as principle and dialogue' (Reidemeister, 1982: 27).

The dialogue could be with the client, other architects in an office situation, critics, architects reached through publication, or a play of give and take specifically with the architect's own mind. The media and techniques architects use depend, often, on their individual philosophy and approach to the design process. Each architect does not necessarily commence each project in exactly the same way, since each project has a specific program and criteria. Conversely, the media or techniques of sketching may direct the way the architects interpret. This, in most cases, would not 'control' the outcome but would certainly affect the visual exercise. Similarly, the media with which architects begin to explore a design have an effect on the finished building. Vincent Scully speculates on this connection when describing the method Paul Rudolph used to design. Rudolph employed a technique of parallel pencil lines to give texture and shade. Scully feels this technique is the reason he used so much vertically striated concrete in his architecture (Pierce, 1967).

Architects' limitations and abilities to manipulate their media affect the outcome of the design. For example, unless the architect has expertise in the operation of CAD, a design using this medium may lack definition and become mediocre because the computer might make rectangles more easily than other shapes. This may be true of skills in any medium. Thus, techniques and media influence what a sketch communicates to architects and, on the other hand, who they want to speak to and what is meant to be said influences the architect's choices concerning media and techniques.

Another purpose for which architects utilize sketches is to record, since the sketch often acts as a memory device. Architects may use sketches as visual notes, to act as travel companions to bring the trip home. This preserving may not necessarily be of the journey's events but could include recording precedent, concepts or associative configurations. The sketches may document likeness of an object or thought, or could capture a monetary idea that may become easily forgotten. Like poetic drawings, the sketch may preserve an emotion or feeling that may not be easily recreated. Such sketches might also be diagrammatic studies, where the thinking through a process or the analysis of an event might be lost without a reminder. These sketches, as memoranda, may act to reserve specific concepts but are not necessarily a visual narrative with symbolic relationships. Since architectural sketches are distinctly individual very few architects use a consistent system of symbols. The two-dimensional images contain a more complex relationship: they hold multiple dimensions of communication.

The last primary function of architectural sketches also involves communication, but in this form it mediates between the architect and the sketch, since architects often use sketches for evaluation. The visual image can be a proposal to be criticized; thus, it can be used for decision-making. Once the sketch is on paper the architect can compare, by a process of perception, its consistency with the mind's eye. Ernst Gombrich describes this as a process of matching and correction (Gombrich, 1984).

The purpose of testing, or visualizing, these designs on paper may be to match a mental likeness, but it can also make a judgment concerning a preconceived notion. An architect may sketch not knowing where the action of sketching will lead, but in reviewing the combination of lines he or she can evaluate the possible solutions. One common description of the design process as problem, solution and critique illustrates this procedure (Broadbent, 1973). As architects criticize their sketches, concepts may become more defined. More specifically, sketches support opportunities for analysis and assist understanding of complex constructs. When sketching to test, architects might make pages of sketches, each with slight variations. It is also possible for the sketch to communicate an impossible solution, which can be quickly seen and subsequently rejected in favor of a whole new assemblage. With the disposable and immediate aspects of sketches, a decision can be made with minimal investment of time.

These four sketches by Merrill Elam (Figures 1.6–1.9), principal in the firm Mack Scogin Merrill Elam Architects, explore a method of visualization. Having worked together for over thirty years, the team's practice has focused primarily on libraries and academic buildings. Based in Atlanta, Georgia, they have been widely published in journals and are also the subject of two monographs. Their buildings have received many honors such as National American Institute of Architects Awards for Excellence, Georgia American Institute of Architects Design of Excellence Awards and several *Architectural Record* House Awards. Their projects include the William C. Blakley Law Library, Arizona State University; the Turner Village at the Candler School of Theology at Emory University; Berkeley Music Library and most recently a United States Courthouse in Austin, Texas, to be completed in 2008.

This series of sketches describes elevations for the Jean Gray Hargrove Music Library. A practice that employs digital technology for conceptual design besides production, this sketch shows tremendous energy and articulation. Each treated slightly differently, the elevations have been outlined in ink and shades of blue and green have been applied. Each has been drawn freehand with remarkably accurate proportion.

The north elevation (Figure 1.6) is distinctive with its strong horizontal lines. It appears that the lines, the horizontal ones in particular, have been reinforced in an effort to either emphasize the connection of the glass or to ensure an accurate and straight representation. Another reason for reinforcing lines could be the result of choosing a pen with a fine nib. It is possible that Elam was expecting to view a heavier articulation of the connector and was repeating the lines to compensate. If this was the case, the visual testing shows a process of immediate evaluation. She may have been imagining a heavier line or could have, in the instant of seeing the sketch emerge, decided a heavier horizontal was more appropriate. Once viewed, decisions could be made.

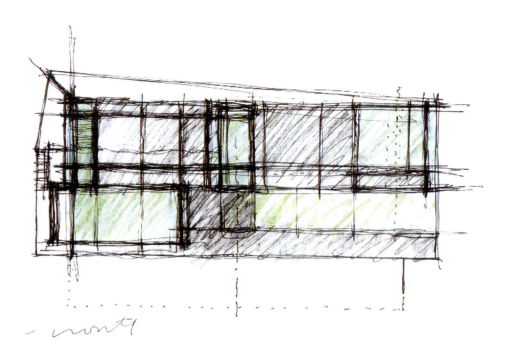

FIGURE 1.6   Merrill Elam; Jean Gray Hargrove Music Library, University of California, Berkeley, North Elevation.

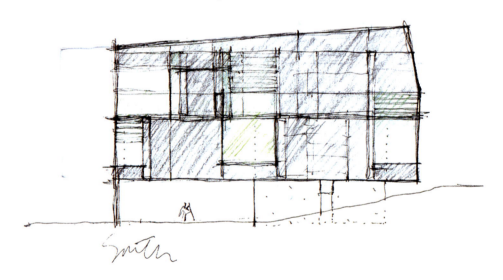

FIGURE 1.7   Merrill Elam; Jean Gray Hargrove Music Library, University of California, Berkeley, South Elevation.

The south elevation (Figure 1.7) is rendered one hue of blue, either more dense or less dense depending upon a level of desired transparency. The ability to layer the colored pencil means Elam could reinforce areas through comparison. Viewing the entire façade provided this opportunity for judgment. The west elevation (Figure 1.8) demonstrates relatively slow lines that wobble only slightly. The ends of many of these lines fold back on themselves where they intersect perpendicular

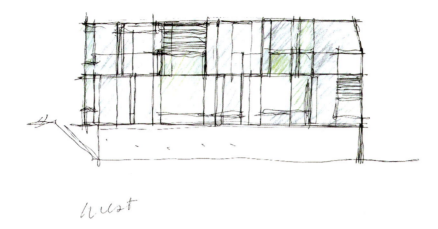

FIGURE 1.8   Merrill Elam; Jean Gray Hargrove Music Library, University of California, Berkeley, West Elevation.

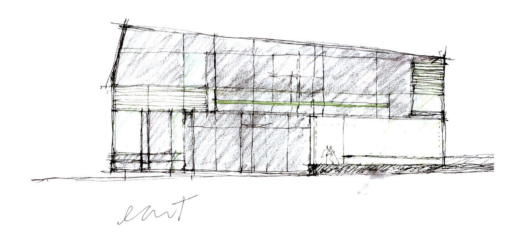

FIGURE 1.9   Merrill Elam; Jean Gray Hargrove Music Library, University of California, Berkeley, East Elevation.

lines. This may be an effort to end the line definitively or it could be an instance where their intersection was important. In the past, drafts people were taught to cross perpendicular lines rather than stop short of their connection. This may be use of body memory, or habit, on the part of Elam.

Each sketch, although using precise ink lines, has strong diagonals to fill in larger areas of color. Appearing to be partially a study of the transparency, translucency, and opaqueness of the façade (Figure 1.9), the various densities create a modeled effect. In these four sketches, Merrill Elam utilizes the sketch to visually evaluate an impression.

To summarize, architects use sketches in many individual ways, but formulating a few general functions can reveal how architects employ them in the design process. Sketches may be a method for discovery, and they also facilitate communication both with colleagues and with the architects themselves. Sketches can assist memory as a visual record of places, emotions, or concepts. The quick sketch may help the architect to make decisions either to test a concept or to match a form in the mind's eye. Again, Filarete describes the potential acquisition of knowledge and the joy of drawing:

Execution teaches many things and everything cannot be fully narrated here…everything that is done by the hand partakes of drawing…it is an unknown and little appreciated science. You would do very well to learn it, for it would acquaint you with a thousand delights. (Filarete, 1965: 82, 149)

BIBLIOGRAPHY

(1971). *Webster's Third International Dictionary.*

(1985). *The Compact Edition of the Oxford English Dictionary.* Oxford University Press.

Akin, Ö. and Weinel, E.F. (1982). *Representation and Architecture.* Information Dynamics.

Alberti, L.B. (1988). *On the Art of Building in Ten Books* (Translated by Rykwert, J., Leach, N. and Tavernor, R.) Massachusetts Institute of Technology Press.

Aristotle, (1951). *Aristotle's Theory of Poetry and Fine Art.* Dover.

Aristotle, (1973). *Aristotle De sensu and De memoria* (Translated by Ross, G.R.T.). Arno Press.

Arnheim, R. (1969). *Visual Thinking.* University of California Press.

Baldinucci, C.F. (1681). *Vocabolario Toscano dell'Arte del Disegno* (Edited 1809). Opere.

Barthes, R. (1988). *The Semiotic Challenge.* Hill and Wang.

Beckmann, J. (1998). *The Virtual Dimension: Architecture, Representation, and Crash Culture.* Princeton Architectural Press.

Bilda, Z. and Gero, J.S. (2005). Does Sketching Off-Load Visuo-Spatial Working Memory? In *Studying Designers '05* (edited by J.S. Gero and N. Bonnardel), pp. 145–159. Key Centre of Design Computing and Cognition, University of Sydney.

Bonta, J.P. (1979). *Architecture and its Interpretation: a Study of Expressive Systems in Architecture.* Rizzoli.

Broadbent, G. (1973). *Design In Architecture.* John Wiley and Sons.

Buchler, J. (ed.) (1955). *Philosophical Writings of Pierce.* Dover Publications.

Calvino, I. (1988). *Six Memos for the Next Millennium.* Harvard University Press.

Collingwood, R.G. (1964). *The Principles of Art.* Oxford University Press.

Coulton, J.J. (1977). *Ancient Greek Architects at Work.* Cornell University Press.

Croce, B. (1970). *Aesthetic.* MacMillan.

Culler, J.D. (1986). *Ferdinand de Saussure.* Cornell University Press.

Dal Co, F. and Mazzariol, G. (1984). *Carlo Scarpa, The Complete Works.* Electa/Rizzoli.

Eco, U. (1976). *A Theory of Semiotics.* Indiana University Press.

Eco, U. (1985). *Faith in Fakes.* Secker and Warburg.

Eco, U. and Sebeck, T.A. (1983). *The Sin of Three: Dupin, Homes, Pierce.* Indiana University Press.

Evans, R. (1986). Translations From Drawing to Building. *AA Files,* **12**, pp. 3–18.

Filarete, (1965). *Treatise on Architecture* (Translated by Spencer, J.R.). Yale University Press.

Fraser, I. and Henmi, R. (1994). *Envisioning Architecture: an analysis of drawing.* Van Nostrand Reinhold.

Fuess, R. (1982). Epiphany: To the First Sketch in Modern Literature. *Daidalos,* **5**, pp. 23–6.

Gadamer, H-G. (1989). *Truth and Method.* Crossroad.

Gibson, J.J. (1979). *The Ecological Approach to Visual Perception.* Houghton Mifflin Company.

Gibson, J.J. (1982). *Reasons for Realism: Selected Essays of James J. Gibson* (Edited by Reed, E. and Jones, R.). Lawrence Erlbaum Associates.

Goel, V. (1995). *Sketches of Thought.* Massachusetts Institute of Technology Press.

Gombrich, E. (1984). *Art and Illusion.* Princeton University Press.

Gombrich, E. (1985). *The Story of Art.* Prentice-Hall.

Heidegger, M. (1962). *Being and Time.* Harper.

Hewitt, M. (1985). Representational Forms and Modes of Conception. *Journal of Architectural Education*, **39/2**, pp. 2–9.

Jung, C.G. (1968). *Man and His Symbols*. Dell.

Kahn, L.I. (1991). *Writings, Lectures, Interviews*. Edited by Latour, A. Rizzoli.

Kearney, R. (1988). *The Wake of the Imagination: toward a postmodern culture*. University of Minnesota Press.

Langer, S.K. (1957). *Problems of Art*. Charles Scribner.

Lauer, D.A. (1979). *Design Basics*. Holt Rinehart and Winston.

Le Corbusier, (1981). *Le Corbusier's Sketchbooks Volumes 1–4*. MIT Press and the Foundation Le Corbusier.

Lethaby, W.R. (1974). *Architecture, Mysticism and Myth*. The Architectural Press.

McQuaid, M. (2000). *Envisioning Architecture: Drawings from the Museum of Modern Art*. University of Minnesota Press.

Meisenheimer, W. (1987). The Functional and the Poetic Drawing. *Daidalos*, **25**, pp. 111–20.

Merleau-Ponty, M. (1962). *Phenomenology of Perception* (Translated by Routledge, C.S. and Kegan, P.) The Humanities Press.

Merleau-Ponty, M. (1964). *Primacy of Perception: and other Essays on Phenomenological Psychology, the Philosophy of Art, History and Politics*. Northwestern University Press.

Mitchell, W.J.T. (1986). *Iconology: Image, Text, Ideology*. The University of Chicago Press.

Hölzinger, J.P. *et al* (1982). Questioned About First Sketches. *Daidalos*, **5**, pp. 35–60.

Oechslin, W. (1982). The Well-Tempered Sketch. *Daidalos*, **5**, pp. 99–110.

Pierce, J.S. (1967). Architectural Drawings and the Intent of the Architect. *Art Journal*, **27**, pp. 48–59.

Piotrowski, A. and Robinson, J.W. (2001). *The Discipline of Architecture*. University of Minnesota Press.

Reidemeister, A. (1982). The Sketch as a Practical Instrument. *Daidalos*, **5**.

Robbins, E. (1994). *Why Architects Draw*. Massachusetts Institute of Technology Press.

Santayana, G. (1961). *The Sense of Beauty, Being the Outline of Aesthetic Theory*. Collier Books.

Schön, D. (1983). *The Reflective Practitioner: How Professionals Think in Action*. Basic Books.

Smith, K.S. (2005). *Architect's Drawings: A Selection of Sketches by World famous Architects Through History*. The Architectural Press.

Sorabji, R. (1972). *Aristotle on Memory*. Duckworth.

Summers, D. (1981). *Michelangelo and the Language of Art*. Princeton University Press.

Suwa, M., Gero, J. and Purcell, T. (1999). Unexpected Discoveries: How Designers Discover Hidden Features in Sketches. In *Visual and Spatial Reasoning in Design* (edited by J.S. Gero and B. Tversley), pp. 1–18. Key Centre of Design Computing and Cognition, University of Sydney, Sydney, Australia.

Tschumi, B. (1994). *Architecture and Disjunction*. Massachusetts Institute of Technology Press.

Vesely, D. (1985). Architecture and the Conflict of Representation. *AA Files*, **8**, pp. 21–38.

Vesely, D. (1987). Architecture and the Poetics of Representation. *Daidalos*, **25**, pp. 24–36.

Walker, J.A. and Chaplin, S. (1977). *Visual Culture*. Manchester University Press.

Wollheim, R. (1971). *Art and Its Objects*. Harper and Row.

Wollheim, R. (1974). *On Art and the Mind*. Harvard University Press.

CHAPTER 2

PLAY, QUICKNESS AND *FESTINA LENTE*

Play is far from being only a child's game. James Hans believes that play is central to living, and he writes of inorganic, organic, and human play. Inorganic and organic objects have a part to play in the world, even if it is a small part. Even a rock plays, although it may wait centuries to become actively involved. It has a part in the order of the universe, which makes it playful within its environment (Hans, 1981). Play constitutes a mode of manipulation and learning; its implementation might provide an approach to truth and interpretation. The framework of play provides boundaries to stretch against and becomes a method of representation. Play itself is an activity in which all humans engage, even when 'working' (Hans, 1981). This discussion of play will begin with the etymology of several words derived from the Latin verb 'to play.' This sets the stage for an examination of the many aspects of human play.

Allusion, illusion, delusion, prelude, and interlude are all variations on the Latin '*ludere*', meaning 'to play'. The prefix of each word changes its meaning somewhat, although each maintains its reference to play. An allusion conveys an indirect mention – an indirect but meaningful reference. It is not an obvious reference; in fact, it may not be comprehended at all. Allusion resembles a private joke or an inside story. It is playful in its dependence on the knowledge of the reader or listener. Allusion has an etymological origin from to 'play with'; on the contrary, illusion is 'against play', and is a deception, trickery, sometimes a false or often erroneous image. It suggests negative connotations of 'a mistaken perception of reality, a mistaken belief or concept' (Oxford English Dictionary). An illusionist image may not allow play or finding the truth through play.

On the other hand, allusion is play; the subtle references and analogies allow the ability to see more clearly, even if that image is less plausible or immediately incomprehensible. Sketches that contain allusions are subtle in their reference; they provoke new thoughts because they contain a fraction, or a connotation, which sparks an atmosphere or memory. The reductive medium characterizes sketches; they can be 'realistic,' but this does not necessarily mean they are documentary. These playful sketches refer to an abstract notion; they are not necessarily restricted to the false phantom of illusion. Thus, the play of the sketch fluctuates somewhere between the *illusion* of definitive 'reality', and the *allusion* of abstraction and limited identity.

A few examples clarify how allusion and illusion can be apparent in architectural sketches. Expressionist architectural sketches of the early part of the twentieth century provided an emotional outlet for the architect's energy. Wolfgang Pehnt explains the significance of the sketch for Expressionist architects: '[w]here the creative urge was so highly valued, the architectural sketch became doubly significant. Sketches promised insight into the creative process, and with their aid artists could tap sources that would otherwise remain buried' (Pehnt, 1985: 6).

FIGURE 2.1　Michel de Klerk; Apartment Block 2, Spaarndammer-plantsoen, Amsterdam, 1914–16.

ILLUSION AND ALLUSION

Michel de Klerk, part of the Expressionist movement, lived and worked in Amsterdam (1884–1923) and provides an example of controlled illusionary sketches. Having worked with Eduard Cuypers, de Klerk built numerous housing projects in Amsterdam, primarily of brick. His projects suggest the English Arts and Crafts movement, but he also used Dutch models.

This page of sketches (Figure 2.1) depicts some qualities of illusion. The sketches of exterior ornament are illusionary images, in that they seem quite three-dimensional, as shadows show depth, and each sketch is carefully drawn to express texture and materials. De Klerk carefully renders detail as he was intimately conscious of how materials would be joined. The many variations overlap in his eagerness to find a solution. He was testing the form against his imagination and judgment. Interestingly, de Klerk finishes each sketch to a degree where it can be evaluated, almost giving each one the opportunity to impress him. Other architects may reject solutions early in the process, when they do not show promise. These sketches are playful in the repetition of forms to locate alternative inventions. More explicitly, the drawing conveys illusionary qualities as the sketch provides a more complete or 'realistic' impression.[1] As there can be time and place for both illusion and allusion, it is not a negative feature, in this case, to be completely descriptive.

Within a definition of play, de Klerk's drawing is not as playful as others that are less descriptive. It lacks the looseness that encourages free associations and may be too definite to support imaginative insight. By contrast, a drawing by the contemporary architect Eric Kahn (Figure 2.2) alludes to many shapes and images. Eric Kahn, with Ron Golan and Russell Thomsen, created the Central Office of Architecture in 1987. They have won awards such as the Young Architects Award and Emerging Voices from the Architectural League of New York. Profoundly interested in architecture as a *tool*, on their website they write that they view it as '…a means to making other means and ends [living, dwelling],…an apparatus for the promotion of humanism.'

With clients such as the Getty Conservation Institute and the Southern California Institute of Architecture, their wide range of built work includes the Brix Restaurant in Venice, California and *La Opinión* in Los Angeles. This page of loose scribbles, an early design sketch entitled *Urban Fabric: Mexico City*, epitomizes allusion. The forms appear to be quick proportioned shapes to spark the imagination in an effort to force associations that could be used later. This sketch, then, becomes a way to continue an allusive dialogue. When asked to describe his relationship with his sketches, Kahn references the thinking evident in a playful dialogue:

> *Sketching is improvising; it is an action that unfolds through time. These sketches are instances of improvisational thinking; they start with a theme based in direct unmediated observation and become improvisations as they drift iteratively.[2] Drawing as thinking emphasizes and leverages its ability as a means (verb) rather than precious ends (nouns). In this sense drawing is a necessary act for the thinking architect, not a romantic indulgence. They exhibit an absolute aesthetic absenteeism; a dialogic mode characterized by the engaged philologist not the interested artist. En masse they are modest recordings they are highly contingent on the impressions left by human circumstance. As research instruments, they coax out of the domain of concealment the charged will of our life – world in a mode proper to it. (Kahn, personal communication)*

On the page can be viewed slow deliberate lines contrasted by faster undulating marks. The speed of the marks shows in how they are wavy, almost becoming like an artist's contour lines. As if produced with a loose hand, they become straighter when grouped together. These lines suggest dimension and become volumes for the articulation of spatial elements seemingly bursting from the interstitial space. The approximately five sketches crowded on the page seem to evoke a movement through space as parallel lines mark distances and length of shadows. Placed as to be analytical, the bundles of sketches evoke compression and release. Alluding to three-dimensional forms, they demand interpretation.

---

[1] 'Realistic' in detail and line proportion, not necessarily dimension or texture. See Umberto Eco (1979) *A Theory of Semiotics*. Interestingly Pehnt writes about the illusionary qualities of de Klerk's work: '…a matter of dimensioning and structural reconsideration as in many of Michel de Klerk's sketches, or where the client had to be provided with a lucid view of his future real estate, the spontaneous gesture was out of place.' (Pehnt, 1985, 8)

[2] Kahn writes: 'The Anatomy of "Observation", focuses on the etymology of the word "observation" itself, as Jonathan Crary illuminated in *Techniques of the Observer*, unlike spectare, the Latin root for "spectator", the root for "observe" does not literally connote "to look at"…observare, means "to conform one's action, to comply with", as in observing rules, codes, regulations, and practices. Though obviously one who sees, an observer is more importantly one who sees within a prescribed set of possibilities, one who is embedded in a system of conventions and limitations. And by "conventions" I mean to suggest far more than representational practices.'

FIGURE 2.2 Eric A. Kahn; Urban Fabric: Mexico City (D.F.) 2003. The morphology
of a fabric city, with its clear distinction of block and street structure drifts towards
'scoring' intervals of street paving, façade rhythms, and light and shadow projections,
unraveling the striated space of the city.

When asked to comment on the sketches, Kahn explains the thoughts that provoked them.
'The morphology of a fabric city, with its clear distinction of block and street structure drifts
towards **scoring** intervals of street paving, façade rhythms, light and shadow projections unraveling
the striated space of the city.' These sketches allude to shadow and structure while conjuring the
imagination. Although a combination of loose and controlled lines, the sketch remains within the
urban theme and, thus, the subject matter defines the limits of the play.

Boundaries are important aspects of a theory of play. The abstract concept of play is reminiscent of the freedom of childhood, but play of any sort has restrictions. Jacques Derrida explains the role of free play by introducing its boundaries; he writes that play is bound in two crucial senses:

[F]irst, the beginning of play is always necessarily connected to a foreproject, to a series of prejudgments that are at issue in the activity of play itself, that give an orientation to the play; and second, the result of play is a structure, a framework or order that has been confirmed by the play itself. (Hans, 1981: 10–11)

As in the context of games, there always exists some adversary, some limit of freedom, to overcome and to act against. It may be an opponent, a rule, a chance (luck), predictability, or a boundary of space, time or physical being (Weinsheimer, 1985). Hans-Georg Gadamer expresses this aspect of play as a kind of determinism when he writes about the action of play: 'no play is perfectly free play…to play is to sacrifice freedom and accept limits…being limited, being played, is a condition of playing at all' (Weinsheimer, 1985: 104).

Hans finds a similar connotation of boundaries or limits in the intention of play. It might be desire that intensifies the search for an architectural solution, for example. 'Desire as I wish to consider it occurs as an aspect of the activity of play. If play is the activity, and production is the result of activity, desire is what provides the orientation and motivation for play' (Hans, 1981: 51). A soccer game would not be very interesting if the goal posts were removed. The rules for an architect – of budget, site, or program – confine the play, and these limits structure the architect's creativity; similarly, a sketch has boundaries in its media and time limits. The sketch is also confined by the architect's skills, mindset, the program of the project, or artificial limits evoked by the designer.

A game, too restricting, has no movement or flexibility; consequently, the play loses interest, and it could be said it has no play. The architectural theorist Marco Frascari expresses this seizing up of play by the example of play versus tolerance in a joint.[3] The joint must contain play in order to move and work. Tolerance is either something required or a mistake, and is not built into or designed to allow for free movement and play. To leave some play means to leave some vagueness. In a similar way, the play adjusts to the game as it is played. A team of soccer players identifies the strongest player on the opposing team, and they modify their play to compensate. They are, in fact, testing the tolerance, and the play generates new structures, not only with and within former frames (Hans, 1981). Through play, the players adapt to a changing world and this change enriches the play. Psychologists refer to this as 'feedback', and many architects use sketches in a similar manner, adjusting the sketches to reflect constant reactions to the images they perceive.

Hans feels that play requires both novelty and repetition and that the course of the play incorporates the relationship between these two: 'play shares one thing with games: a familiar structure that allows one to play with the unfamiliar' (Hans, 1981: 28). The difference adds to the knowledge and interest of the game, for if the soccer game was played exactly the same way each time, the winner would be obvious and all involved would quickly lose interest. Hans further states that the repetition provides structure, but that change depends upon orientation: '[t]his structure of the familiar then permits the introduction of the different; play in one sense is no more than the infection of the familiar by difference' (Hans, 1981: 28).

All play involves this departure of difference, since play is never static and the intensity changes with each activity. Hans provides an example from art: '[a]esthetic activity can sometimes generate an intensity which would seem to approach the intensity of an orgasm or a religious experience, but at other times aesthetic experience might generate effects which could only be characterized as mildly pleasing' (Hans, 1981: 40). The play depends upon continuity since the imitation often breaks loose to a diversity which may or may not be vivid (Hans, 1981: 44).

---

[3] From a seminar conducted by Dr. Marco Frascari at Georgia Tech (Spring 1988).

Diversity often relies upon the give and take of play. Again, in a soccer game each play requires a reaction and the play continues on subsequent actions. It is difficult to play ball totally alone, unless there is some challenge to react against. Kick, toss, and volley are analogies from games that elucidate this mental activity. Architects employ a similar technique when playing back and forth with a sketch since the repetition of the sketch, along with its variation, continues the play of designing.

It becomes necessary, at this point, to differentiate the sketch and a 'game'. The amount of intentionality might be at issue because compared to a game, the sketch may not have as clear an objective. The give and take of play resembles the delicate balance between fight and fun. This challenge in the play of children hones their skills and replicates other challenges (Lieberman, 1977). There is a fine line which separates these two; often, what starts as fun turns to fight and vice versa. A question arises here: what activity constitutes play?

Hans asks this question and agrees with Gadamer that it can be said '[p]lay fulfills its purpose only if the player loses himself in play' (Gadamer, 1989: 102). Play focuses on activity, not objects (Hans, 1981). Gadamer writes that the players become so engrossed in their action that what is seen is the 'primacy of play over the consciousness of the player' (Gadamer, 1989: 104). In fact the play only exists during the activity of being played:

The players are not the subjects of the play; instead play merely reaches presentation through the players...all playing is a being-played. (Gadamer, 1989: 103, 106)

It is as if the player forfeits power to the game and, subsequently, the player has the experience of 'being outside oneself'. The play is all-absorbing, and Hans sees the activity of play as unselfconscious (Hans, 1981). Other philosophers who write about play reinforce this concept in their own terms. Johann Huizinga writes about play as being 'captivating' and 'enchanting' (Huizinga, 1955). Gilles Deleuze and Felix Guattori reiterate this thought: 'the unconscious only becomes another word for play' (Hans, 1981: 61). If play enchants the player and that player is not consciously thinking of him or herself, then the activity of the play can combine recent experience and blend fields of play together.

The connection of experiences into play activity involves memory, imagination, and fantasy all within a framework:

[T]he activity of play is neither unconsciousness or self-reflexive, but it nevertheless depends on both in the following manner. All playful activity is given some kind of shape by what has preceded it. That shape is never easily definable, but we can say that in many cases active syntheses are a part of that shape. In playing with an idea, one might well begin by questioning the relation between the arts and sciences and by positing any number of features which might correspond to each. (Hans, 1981: 59)

Once again it is possible to use the analogy of a game of soccer, where the players combine experience and intelligence to play the game. This activity involves knowledge of the rules, body coordination, strategy, cognitive anticipation, and memory, to name just a few. The connections between thoughts and events could be seen as similar to association, where one thing leads to another in an often unusual and surprising combination. Likewise, architects use all of these activities. They are educated in the rules, approach the activity of sketching with intention, and utilize all their faculties of intelligence, imagination and memory.

The activity of play also entails 'representation-of' and 'representation-for' (Weinsheimer, 1985; Wollheim, 1971). The choice provided for the player can either take on a role or play the play for meaning. 'Representation-of' is self-representation, where a player is acting a part. The player could be a member of a team or an actor in a theatrical production. 'Representation-for' overlaps this but takes on symbolic connotations. Gregory Bateson describes play for cultural representation: 'the actions of "play" are related to, or denote, other actions of "not play". We, therefore, meet in play with an instance of signals standing for other events, and it appears, therefore, that the evolution of play may have been an important step in the evolution of communication' (Bateson, 1972: 181).

Gregory Bateson uses the playful activity of puppies to examine some of the representations of play. Puppies play at biting each other, but each knows that it is play, and if one of them nips too hard, they yelp and realize it is no longer play. The relationship is not one to one, as the nip does not replace the bite but represents it. '[T]hese actions, in which we now engage, do not denote what would be denoted by those actions which these actions denote...The playful nip denotes the bite, but it does not denote what would be denoted by the bite' (Bateson, 1972: 181). For an architect, the sketch does not directly replace the building, which is merely in its conceptual stages, but the architect plays with these sketches knowing that they are only a 'nip' of that building. Although the sketch cannot physically react it might seem to; consequently sketches are not always 'controllable'.

A KNOWLEDGE GAINED

The experiences of play alter our mode of thinking. There remains a learning process involving interpretation that results in the production of play (Hans, 1981). 'The why of play is quite obvious: one seeks to play because one believes that the understanding achieved through play is more valuable than the kinds of understanding achieved in other ways' (Hans, 1981: 11–12). Play helps to view issues in a new light, because the many opportunities to interpret give the play meaning. Especially in an art-form, where there is never a single understanding, the work in play cannot be misunderstood. Impossible to predict what will be achieved or learned from the game, this knowledge has many possible meanings, and this becomes its life. As Hans writes, play can help to understand problems:

> *Man may have a purpose in his play, but this purpose is always no more than an orientation if his play really is to be play. Man may play with certain ideas in the hope of resolving a particular problem, but if he is really playing with the ideas, the play of ideas directs him rather than the other way around. (Hans, 1981: 32)*

The act of sketching is play; the sketches themselves are not. The give and take of play constitutes the dialogue between architects and their pencils. As with children, the structuring role of play increases knowledge and influences comprehension. Colin St. John Wilson, in his article on play, discusses the function of aesthetic play in acquiring knowledge:

> *Hans-Georg Gadamer has given an extended philosophical treatment of the structuring role of aesthetic play resulting in a form of knowledge...And just as for Aquinas and the Schoolmen, art was that which draws out the particular clarity of something, 'the beauty of intelligibility'. (St. John Wilson, 1986: 17)*

Similarly, broken rules often allow designers to perceive more possibilities. Dialogue, in a playful situation with paper and an easily manipulated media, provides a key element in our ability to 'think' with a pencil (Huizinga, 1955).

With a sketch, as is the case with a piece of artwork, the duplication presents a new and different emphasis. Mechanical reproduction, or any kind of duplication, precludes play since the creative excitement lost through replication is irretrievable. This process cannot be repeated, and what the architect discovered does not need to be 'found out' again. It would be tautological to attempt the sketches again, as the thought has been absorbed or built upon once. Hans-Georg Gadamer writes about form, referring to the repeatability of play, especially a theatrical play. As the play becomes repeatable and permanent, it loses the qualities of a game: '[t]hus, transformation into structure means that what existed previously exists no longer. But also that what now exists, what represents itself in the play of art, is the lasting and true' (Gadamer, 1989: 111).

The action of play pertaining to architectural sketches could be compared to dance. Until a dance is performed, it is only a script for a dance. If the players stop it is no longer a dance, and the performers do not form dance until they partake in the action of dancing (Weinsheimer, 1985: 108). Sketching has this immediacy since, when the play completes, the object is less valuable. A sketch's importance depends on the course of the play because, in the process of design, the project evolves into another stage of precise drawings. The sketch loses its magic and has no importance after the result of the play is revealed and the architect's mind stops interacting with it. Most often the architect builds a model or progresses to measured drawings and the sketches are disposed of. This could be one reason why very few architectural sketches remain from the past.

PLAY AT WORK

Before looking at a few examples of architectural sketches it seems appropriate to conclude with a quote suitable to the discussion of play. These thoughts by Huizinga succinctly express the knowledge and joy that can be acquired through play:

> *Let us enumerate once more the characteristics we deemed proper to play. It is an activity which proceeds within certain limits of time and space, in a visible order, according to rules freely accepted, and outside the sphere of necessity or material utility. The play-mood is one of rapture and enthusiasm, and is sacred or festive in accordance with the occasion. A feeling of exultation and tension accompanies the action, mirth and relaxation follow. (Huizinga, 1955: 132)*

A page of sketches for the design of the Dipoli Student Assembly Building in Ontaniemi, Espoo, Finland, by Reima Pietilä (Figure 2.3), exemplifies an architect's playful use of sketches. The Finnish architect Pietilä, with foundations in Modernism, describes his work as 'organic'. His often undulating shapes reflect his interest in the 'phenomenology of place'. A few of his most celebrated projects include the Finnish Embassy in New Delhi, India; the Kaleva Church in Tampere, Finland; and the Metso, the Tampere Main Library. Impossible to witness the play when completed, these sketches act as the remnants left from designing that provide a record of the activity of play.

The first noticeable issue of play finds that the sketches are definitely not static, since they undulate with the variation of lines. Some lines seem slow and deliberate, but most display the fervor of activity as they overlap and reinforce the areas of concentration. This page includes heavy moving and sometimes wavy, contour lines. There is also the evidence of fast straight lines, some with tails curved in anticipation of the next swift mark. Play is not static, and the quick-moving diagonal definitive lines keep one's eyes moving across the page. These lines reflect an exuberance distinctive of play.

The placement of the sketches appears haphazard, since they are scattered in enthusiasm across the page. Rather than being sequential, they are tightly placed and almost overlap each other. Being in various states of incompleteness, it is feasible to imagine that Pietilä judged an abstract concept unsuccessful and abandoned it to start a new thought. The random placement of the sketches suggests his intense concentration and may lead a viewer to believe he was truly playing by losing himself in playful activity. Drawing over a line might be a way to reinforce an edge or boundary, which may indicate it was deemed correct. Another reason an architect would draw over lines might be in order to prolong the drawing process, thus giving the architect time to think about the next form or decision.

Pietilä's play remains loose and expressive, but he never crosses the boundary to explore anything other than this building. In a mode typical of play, he has chosen an orientation and stretches

FIGURE 2.3   Reima Pietilä; Dipoli Student Assembly Building, Ontaniemi, Espoo.

the rules within these confines. By altering shape, orientation and groupings he tests possibilities of the form. For Pietilä these quick lines are representative, yet not completely literal, of three-dimensional space. He was imagining himself in the building through the activity of the sketch.

The numerous floor plans and elevations contain a certain similarity in their approach. As Pietilä repeats a general theme, each attempt is different. This technique typifies play activity; the play does not replicate the former image but is transformed to allow the unusual – the next step from the usual. Pietilä learns as he sketches, and he tests the 'tolerance' to decide on a solution. He uses all of his past experience to modify and translate a form, and as he draws he is making connections in the plays.

An example of sketches by Borromini displays other aspects of play. Francesco Borromini (1599–1667) was a Baroque architect of such buildings as *S. Carlo alle Quattro Fontane* and this is a series of sketches for a gateway arch for that church (Figure 2.4). Upon first observation they appear to be staid precise drawings. The gateways show variations on a theme that sets a framework for the play. Even though carefully drawn, they each contain differences within the usual. It appears Borromini redraws the design over and over, but each example contains the slight, characteristic change of play. These images are playful in a less hurried way. Pietilä's sketches show the fervor of getting lost in activity; on the contrary, Borromini's sketches reveal a slower doodling, which may reflect the artist being lost in concentration. These are definitely sketches because of their freehand quality, but they also reveal a play activity beyond the absent-minded scribbling of mere doodling. The sketches are placed haphazardly on the page, but each is placed on a ground line for orientation. In a playful way, the sketches move off the lower edge of the page.

A striking issue pertaining to this page of sketches is the meaning they communicate to Borromini for decision-making. One gateway is drawn darker in emphasis, in contrast to the other lighter unfinished designs. This is probably the image which he has chosen as the most successful solution, because the others are crossed out with x's. It also has a star inside the arch with some writing, which gives it emphasis. In this way Borromini is concluding the play by choosing a solution for his work.

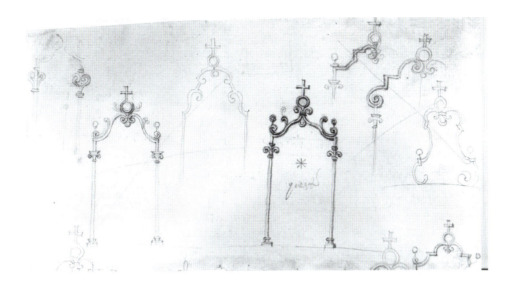

FIGURE 2.4   Francesco Borromini; Gateway for *S. Carlo alle Quattro Fontane*.

Sketches are productive in that the unknown can be 'found' through their activity. Unlike a finished work of art, they are valuable only through their action. They are effortless, and the player can easily become lost in the play. Sketches are swift, which is playful, not pondering. They can be representations-for or representations-of, or be a game in themselves. Roger Caillois writes that some games are played for 'real' and are not representations (Caillois, 1961). Sketches may be play in themselves, possibly employed to obtain an abstract idea rather than to represent a building. They can be 'uncertain' and 'make-believe,' and 'not serious,' but they can also be 'serious' in their ability to assist in the activity of increasing knowledge.

Play involves a player's absorbing interaction with the activity of play. Through allusion, play can give distinct insight into perception. The action of sketching encourages this playful mode which helps the architect to think. Play involves boundaries to stretch against, all-absorbing interaction, repetition and change. Another aspect which is distinctive of play is an element of quickness, i.e. wit, humor and speed.

QUICKNESS AND *FESTINA LENTE*[4]

'Quickness' pertains to a concept examined by Italo Calvino in his book *Six Memos for the Next Millennium* (Calvino, 1988). A term difficult to define simply, it involves economy of expression, time as relative, swift reasoning and consciousness. The issues of quickness resemble play in many

---

[4] *Festina lente* 'make haste slowly' first appeared in the big Aldine edition of 1508. Erasmus writes '…no other proverb is as worthy as this one', and cites an expression from Aristophana, '…make haste hastily', which was altered later. Octavius Caesar is known to have used the phrase repeatedly. Emperor Titus had a coin stamped bearing a dolphin and an anchor, which could illustrate this dichotomy. Erasmus offers three overlapping interpretations of this royal adage: first, 'it would be better to wait a little before tackling a matter; when a decision has been reached, then swift action can be taken'; second, 'the passions of the mind should be reined in by reason'; third, 'precipitate action should be avoided in everything'. Lyons, J.D., and Nichols, S.G. (eds) (1982), pp. 132–148.

ways. The concentration which allows the ability to lose oneself in play is seen in the 'relationship between physical speed and speed of the mind' (Calvino, 1988: 41). Quickness also compares to play in the manipulation of continuity and discontinuity of time, through which it also can enhance learning through activity (Calvino, 1988: 37). Quickness in terms of relative time describes a quality appropriate to sketches, as they are momentary ideas, fast explorations, and immediate imagery. Quickness involves the speed of the sketch, but also the fast mental connections which give meaning to the play of sketching. These sketches are 'quick' in the sense of meaning 'intelligent and witty'.

Calvino starts his chapter on quickness with a story of Charlemagne and a magic ring that commands love or passion.

> *Late in life the Emperor Charlemagne fell in love with a German girl. The barons at his court were extremely worried when they saw that the sovereign, wholly taken up with his amorous passion and unmindful of his regal dignity, was neglecting the affairs of state. When the girl suddenly died, the courtiers were greatly relieved – but not for long, because Charlemagne's love did not die with her. The emperor had the embalmed body carried to his bed chamber, where he refused to be parted from it. The Archbishop Turpin, alarmed by this macabre passion, suspected an enchantment and insisted on examining the corpse. Hidden under the girl's dead tongue he found a ring with a precious stone set in it. As soon as the ring was in Turpin's hands, Charlemagne fell passionately in love with the archbishop and hurriedly had the girl buried. In order to escape the embarrassing situation, Turpin flung the ring into Lake Constance. Charlemagne thereupon fell in love with the lake and would not leave its shores. (Calvino, 1988: 31)*

Calvino highlights in this story an example of the narrative link of folk tales and fairy tales. The rhythm of the story forms a repetitious framework that changes only slightly as it reappears. Each episode of the play instigates a change into the familiar, to stretch the boundaries of the framework. He finds continuity between the different forms of attraction, a theme which bounds the orientation for the play and may be analogous to the framework of an architect's sketch.

The narration of a story avoids unnecessary details but stresses repetition (Calvino, 1988: 35). This repetition marks time, but narrative time is relative; similarly, in the play of a sketch time may pass more quickly or more slowly than actual time, depending upon the concentration. The sketch constitutes a physical remnant of the activity, but it is impossible to exactly comprehend a piece of time. The architect's quality of lines can provide clues to the speed of the drawing, and the nodes of repetitive narration indicate a sequential time.

The activity of quickness indicates life. The quickly drawn, expressive sketch has life; consequently, this movement is reminiscent of a quickening. Marco Frascari discusses a quickening that, traditionally, expresses the first kick of a developing baby inside its mother; subsequently, like the architectural sketch, it represents the movement that indicates life.[5]

On a sketch by Jun Itami (Figure 2.5) it is written how drawing exposes life in the architect's hand. The Japanese architect and artist, Jun Itami, has had a strong foundation in Modernism. He has built such projects as the Hermitage of Inkil in Tokyo, and the Duson Museum and the Stone Museum both in Jeju-do, Korea. Highly celebrated, Itami has been honored with the *Asian Award for Culture and Landscape of Settlements*, International Designing Competition in Asian City Housing and Environment in 2006, and the Award of the Korea Institute of Architects in 2001.

The book, *Drawings by Japanese Contemporary Architects* (Akahira, K. [ed.], 1982), displays a unique group of architectural drawings. In some cases the drawings are sketches, but these images are unusual in that they have been accompanied by words from the respective architects. What is written consists of a statement specifically about the project or the inspiration for the drawing. Either intention or the thoughts of the architect during sketching can be viewed in this unprecedented collection.

---

[5] From a seminar by Dr. Marco Frascari at Georgia Tech, 1989.

FIGURE 2.5   Jun Itami; Stone House 1982.

Pertaining to his sketches Jun Itami writes: 'I want to treasure the characteristic peculiarity of my finger motions, and insist on its value. Its points and continuity, and the discontinuous interceptions transmit the architectural details to the hands. These are all a means of life, like the heartbeat'. Itami sees the life-giving aspect of drawing coming through his hands (his body) and writes, '*drawings* are the traces of hands that endeavor to regain humane architecture' (Akahira, 1982: 32–33).

The page of sketches appears relatively quick in terms of time and efficiency. The building has been outlined and presented with very few lines. In the upper right-hand corner of the sketch, the profile has been completed with one continuous line. This precision reflects tremendous control by the architect and also suggests that it was drawn from a strong image in his mind's eye. Part of the intelligence seen in this sketch emerges from the rendering of a form both complete and descriptive of its materiality. In a sketch with so few lines, it is remarkable to view the masonry heaviness that immediately comes to mind.

The sketch also evokes a certain wit in the references to Le Corbusier. It is possible that once the building emerged on the page, Itami may have realized the similarity in form and added the eye/hand symbol that repeats through Le Corbusier's drawings. The reference to another architect's work shows humor, wit and the intelligence of memory. The section is equally revealing since the profile and ground plane are deftly described using only a few lines. The life of the drawing is indicated by quick expressive lines that are memories of the hands (body) involved.

Although the simple sketch expresses life with precise but active lines, this sketch is not necessarily less informative than others. The sketch does not need to be ponderously stated or depicted to be definite. Sketches are both economic and precise; a quick sketch uses minimal lines to express a truth. Economy refers to using the minimum of anything that can accomplish the purpose, and Calvino reinforces this by writing that folk tales are distinguished by structure, 'economy, rhythm

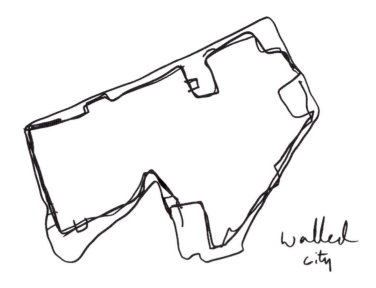

FIGURE 2.6   Floris Alkemade; Zeche Zollverein Masterplan, 2008.

and hard logic' (Calvino, 1988: 35). A few examples demonstrate how quick lines can designate precise meaning.

This sketch from The Office for Metropolitan Architecture in Rotterdam, The Netherlands, (Figure 2.6) discloses the economy of lines used to describe a whole figure. This architectural practice was founded in 1980 by Rem Koolhaas, Elia Zenghelis, Zoe Zenghelis and Madelon Vriesendorp in London, and they have completed innovative works of architecture around the world. Koolhaas was awarded the Pritzker Prize for architecture in 2000 and the 2004 RIBA Gold Medal. They have completed a variety of projects such as the Seoul National University Museum of Art, the Seattle Central Library, the McCormick Tribune Campus Center, Chicago, and the Royal Dutch Embassy in Berlin.

With barely three continuous lines, this sketch is able to describe the parameters of a walled city, showing the profile relationship of inside to outside. These slow confident lines describe the *poché* of the interstitial space between the outline of the outer surfaces and the lines of the inner profile. Interestingly, they question the volume of the enclosed space through the way they vary in distance from each other. The space left between the lines even suggests the materials of construction, both masonry and rectilinear. These precise, observing, and telling lines convey much about the conception of the structure and also allow the architect to envision the edifice.

The next sketch by Robert Venturi (Figure 2.7) for a house in Northern Delaware employs very few lines to create a façade composition in its entirety. Venturi and his wife Denise Scott Brown have been practicing in Philadelphia. He began with the Venturi's Vanna Venturi House in 1962 and since that time their practice, Venturi Scott Brown Architects, has completed a wide range of architectural and urban planning projects. A few examples include Tsinghua University Campus Planning; the Anlyan Center for Medical Research and Education at Yale University; and the Baker/Berry Library and Carson Hall at Dartmouth College. Recipients of numerous awards for their work, they are also educators having written the seminal book *Learning from Las Vegas* (Venturi *et al*, 1977).

With beautifully controlled lines, slow and precise, the proportions and details reveal Venturi's intention. The lines appear to be drawn freehand but the evenness of the medium provides each element of the sketch with equal emphasis. This intelligent sketch speaks of historical reference, materials, and the layering of volume with remarkably few marks. It is possible to speculate that the column centered under the window was drawn first. The other two columns received bumps to represent bases. It appears that after the sketch was complete it needed these 'bumps' added to

FIGURE 2.7   Robert Venturi; House in Northern Delaware.

FIGURE 2.8   Lorcan O'Herlihy; Idea sketch for Landmark Tower / U2 studio in
Dublin, Ireland.

be unified with the later ones. Whatever the actual sequence, this sketch presents the desire for a classical column using a minimal number of lines. The economy of lines and truthful reference causes this sketch to resemble a caricature.

An austere but revealing sketch exemplifies the quick precise lines which so elegantly find the essence of a building. This second sketch from Lorcan O'Herlihy (Figure 2.8) describes an idea for the Landmark Tower/U2 studio in Dublin, Ireland. The economy of lines discloses a quickness that is fast, yet still intelligent and witty. Here the 'relationship between physical speed and speed of the mind' helps O'Herlihy lose himself in the play. The profile of the tower has been defined by just two lines, one of which starts on the left and with bold marks wraps up the side of the tower, across the top, down the other side, and across the bottom. This continuous line changed direction without interruption and surprisingly without emphasizing the corners. A few horizontal marks define the surface articulation of this building. The wavy S's could represent the river flowing through Dublin and, if so, these three lines convey the buildings context. Substantially brief, this image describes the information necessary to visualize the project and thus the quickness.

Calvino, writing about Galileo and his respect for quickness, reiterates this thought. 'For [Galileo], good thinking means quickness, agility in reasoning, economy in argument, but also the use of imaginative examples' (Calvino, 1988: 43). As a comparison, caricature leaves out unnecessary details yet still finds conclusions not clearly depicted and follows every concept to its end (Calvino, 1988). Here, a visual representation can tell more 'truth' than a realistic depiction.

Another concept that helps illuminate the meaning of quickness is *festina lente*. Calvino takes *festina lente* as his personal motto, which translated literally means 'hurry slowly'. 'Hurry slowly', an apparent contradiction, may assist in understanding quickness, since the opposite or mirror reflection can induce a greater understanding. A chiasm has the power to provide a new view; for

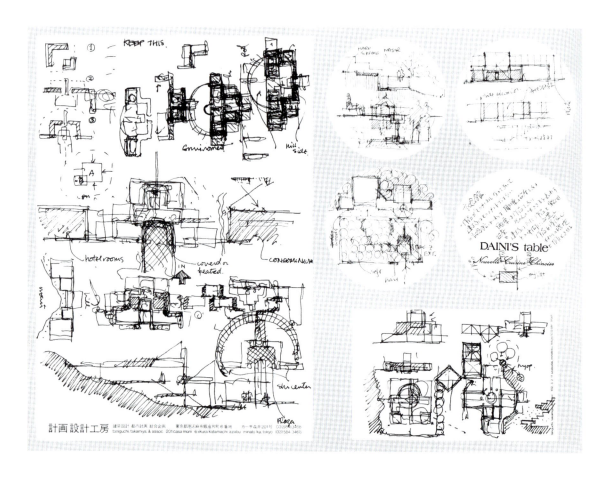

FIGURE 2.9   Yoshio Taniguchi; Seishun Shirakaba Art Museum (Esquisse of the Ken Domon Memorial Hall of Photography).

example, 'the drawing of building and the building of drawing'. In a similar way this reversal can be both precise and imprecise at the same time, depending on how it is viewed.

The above sketches by Venturi and O'Herlihy may appear imprecise, but these sparse lines precisely exhibit a meaning. A Pointillist painting is another example; viewed closely the dots of primary colors are confusing abstractions, but when viewed from a distance the dots become recognizable patterns. The dichotomous terms of *festina lente* make new connections in a way similar to the activity of play, a way that could be described as '...tracing the lightning flashes of the mental circuits that capture and link points distant from each other in space and time' (Calvino, 1988: 48).

This discussion evokes an example, by a Japanese architect, that may illustrate Calvino's conjecture linking distant points. A sketch from the aforementioned book about Japanese contemporary drawings offers insight into an architect's approach to sketching. Figure 2.9, a sketch by Yoshio Taniguchi, is described by the caption '[m]y sketches consist of two kinds, aims and methods of which are contrary to each other...Each of them seems to perform its function of input and output to my architectural design'. An accomplished architect, Taniguchi is best known for his most recent commission to redesign the Museum of Modern Art in New York City. Having worked with Kenzo Tange when younger, a few of his other distinguished projects include the Nagano Prefectural Museum and the Toyota Municipal Museum of Art.

Here Taniguchi seems to be trying to link contrary thoughts in order to give the total meaning. The caption implies play in that the mention of input and output is reminiscent of a scientific accounting, but it also implies a give and take of the two opposite modes. Play exposes this sketch, as the architect gets so lost in the play that the '...sketches can be understood by nobody except me' (Akahira, 1982: 92). Taniguchi appears to resolve issues from contradictory positions to find meaning in his designs.

The contrasting and complementary qualities of *festina lente* are emphasized by Calvino as the characteristics of two Greek gods. 'Vulcan's concentration and craftsmanship are needed to record Mercury's adventures and metamorphoses. Mercury's swiftness and mobility are needed to make Vulcan's endless labors become bearers of meaning' (Calvino,1988, 54). These apparent opposites complement each other, and provide a greater result than they each would separately. With this in mind, Calvino relates another story that is especially important to *festina lente* in the study of sketches:

> *Among Chuang-tzu's many skills, he was an expert draftsman. The king asked him to draw a crab. Chuang-tzu replied that he needed five years, a country house, and twelve servants. Five years later the drawing was still not begun. 'I need another five years', said Chuang-tzu. The king granted them. At the end of these ten years, Chuang-tzu took up his brush and, in an instant, with a single stroke, he drew a crab, the most perfect crab ever seen. (Calvino,1988: 54)*

'Hurry slowly' has meaning for the preparation of the artist/architect. The skills learned and perfected require time because the knowledge to draw something as simple as a crab takes years of cultivation. To make a sketch as brief and thoughtful as the sketches in Figures 2.7 and 2.8 necessitates years of observation and an immense control of the drawing medium. The beauty and truth of simplicity come from experience.

Reminiscent of those who use these skills to impress a client, architects will listen to all comments and often sketch a solution in the presence of that client. This serves several purposes: first, to convince the client that his or her comments are being considered; and secondly, to astonish the client with the architect's skill. Even if the design was carefully worked out in the office weeks before the meeting, the participation with the immediate image completed quickly, and appearing spontaneous, elaborates the dialogue. Here the sketch provides purpose quite different than that of a design sketch. Although not an altogether predictable process, prior study of the subject influences the final connections. Distinctly for show and communication, these sketches reveal the skills of quickness in a precise way.

In a related way, the Japanese artist Hokusai writes about the experience that comes from time and age. His words capture an interesting aspect of quickness in a discussion of time as relative:

From the age of six I had a mania for drawing the shapes of things. When I was fifty I had published a universe of designs. But all I have done before the age of seventy is not worth bothering with. At seventy-five I have learned something of the pattern of nature, of animals, of plants, of trees, birds, fish and insects. When I am eighty you will see real progress. At ninety I shall have cut my way deeply into the mystery of life itself. At a hundred I shall be a marvelous artist. At a hundred and ten everything I create, a dot, a line, will jump to life as never before. To all of you who are going to live as long as I do, I promise to keep my word. I am writing this in my old age. I used to call myself Hokusai, but today I sign myself 'The-Old-Man-Mad-About-Drawing'. (Longstreet, 1969: introduction)

It is interesting that Hokusai said that when he reaches one hundred and ten, the things he draws will jump to life. The goal of drawing for Hokusai was to make that which is inanimate breath – to be inspired with life.

Quickness consists of mental speed and *festina lente*, as it contains the dichotomy of fast and slow, and reveals an intelligence of quickness. 'A swift piece of reasoning is not necessarily better than a long-pondered one. Far from it. But it communicates something special that is derived simply from its very swiftness' (Calvino, 1988: 45).

Architectural sketches contain within them elements of play. Play is not the object but the activity. Since sketches are an activity most often disposed of after the action and knowledge was obtained, they become the mode for thinking, learning and visual manipulation. Quickness adds to play the connotation of speed to connect 'Vulcan's concentration and craftsmanship with Mercury's adventures and metamorphoses'. All of these qualities require the architect's hand on the pencil, playing with the drawing surface.

BIBLIOGRAPHY

(1971). *The Compact Edition of the Oxford English Dictionary.* Oxford University Press.
Akahira, K. (ed.) (1982). *Drawings by Japanese Contemporary Architects.* Graphic-sha Publishing.
Barasch, M. (1985). *Theories of Art, From Plato to Winckelmann.* New York University Press.
Bateson, G. (1972). *Steps to an Ecology of Mind.* University of Chicago Press.
Caillois, R. (1961). *Man, Play and Games.* The Free Press.
Calvino, I. (1988). *Six Memos for the Next Millennium.* Harvard University Press.
Eco, U. (1979). *Theory of Semiotics.* Indiana University Press.
Gadamer, H.-G. (1989). *Truth and Method.* Crossroad.
Hans, J.S. (1980). Hermeneutics, Play, Deconstruction. *Philosophy Today*, Winter.
Hans, J.S. (1981). *The Play of the World.* University of Massachusetts Press.
Huizinga, J. (1955). *Homo Ludens: A Study of the Play Element in Culture.* Beacon Press.
Kris, E. and Kurz, O. (1979). *Legend, Myth and Magic in the Image of the Artist.* Yale University Press.
Lieberman, J.N. (1977). *Playfulness: Its Relationship to Imagination and Creativity.* Academic Press.
Longstreet, S. (1969). *The Drawing of Hokusai.* Bordon Publishing.
Lyons, J.D. and Nichols, S.G. (eds) (1982). *Mimesis: From Mirror to Method.* University Press of New England.
Pehnt, W. (1985). *Expressionist Architecture in Drawing.* Van Nostrand Reinhold Company.
St. John Wilson, C. (1986). The Play of Use and the Use of Play. *Architectural Review*, 180, p. 1073.
Venturi, R., Scott Brown, D. and Izenour, S. (1977). *Learning From Las Vegas: The Forgotten Symbolism of Architectural Form.* MIT Press.
Weinsheimer, J.C. (1985). *Gadamer's Hermeneutics: A Reading of 'Truth and Method'.* Yale University Press.
Wittkower, R. and Wittkower, M. (1963). *Born Under Saturn: the Character and Conduct of Artists: A Documented History from Antiquity to the French Revolution.* Random House.
Wollheim, R. (1971). *Art and Its Objects.* Harper and Row.

CHAPTER 3

MEMORY, IMAGINATION AND FANTASY

In a discussion of architectural representation, it is appropriate to include the faculties of memory, imagination, and fantasy as fundamental components of sketching. Each has a specific identity, but they are also inter-dependent. Memory is a part of our conscious and subconscious mind; it is impossible to escape its presence and influence, thus, it has significant influence upon imagination and fantasy (Casey, 1976). A common definition of imagination as an autonomous mental act includes the power of the mind to form a mental image or concept of something that is unreal or not present. This definition is important in understanding architectural sketching as a creative endeavor, because not knowing how mental impressions originate leads creative people not to speculate, but to proclaim that they came from imagination. Imagination, whose main abilities include a lack of determinism of 'pure possibility', is related to memory and fantasy as an influence or a possible mode of origination (Casey, 1976). Common usage interprets fantasy as creative imagination, or as dramatic fiction marked by highly fanciful or supernatural elements. Fantasy can also be connected to illusion or hallucination. Historically, faculties of memory, imagination and fantasy were seen as being dependent upon images.

The myth of the beginning of drawing provides a good example of image presentation (Evans, 1986). As an attempt to remember her departing lover, Diboutades traces the likeness of him on a wall. Diboutades could have been reminded of her lover in many different ways, but she chose to *keep him* with an image of his person, specifically his body (this may also be the mythical origin of memory, the fragment to keep the memory). Through history the form of the body is magically part of our being. Diboutades did not keep a lock of her lover's hair or copies of his finger prints, instead she retained a tracing of his shadow as an *indication* of his person. Thus, using the recollection faculty of memory, the recombination and image-making qualities of imagination, and the future-creating aspect of fantasy, the myth of Diboutades questions how images take on a speculative role in the early understanding of the faculties of the mind.

Architectural sketches retain a certain amount of mystery because of their tenuous connection to memory, imagination and fantasy. Similar to artists' works, architects' sketches flow from an inner stimulus often seen as magical. Alien to the layman, the sketch is a conceptual 'working through' process for design. Beginning with the topic of memory, continuing with imagination and ending with fantasy, this chapter discusses ways in which these elements are intertwined and cannot be seen as entirely separate. Examples of architects' sketches from history, and those of contemporary architects, will elucidate the roles of memory, imagination and fantasy in the design process.

MEMORY

Memory for humans cannot be escaped, for it is part of all activities. With memory, it is possible to retain knowledge, to use its properties combined with imagination to spark ideas, and to look into the future from past experience. Memory is something called upon for knowledge and, as reminiscing, emerges without much effort (Aristotle, 1928). Being a complex cognitive activity, memory is a necessity in the process of drawing. Sketches, likewise, are dependent upon memory, since thoughts, images and experiences are all part of the architect's whole being and determine what the sketch will be. For example, body memory, interpretation and even specific items that are retained in memory over other experiences influence what an architect sketches.

At one time memory was viewed as a perceptual imprint on the mind. Plato has described this mnemonic imprint as being similar to a stamp or carving on a wax tablet (Plato, 1953). This concept relies heavily on its relationship to perception, as historically an imprint, and was viewed as a permanent or physical phenomena. Plato appears to lack respect for imagination and elevates memory when discussing (in the form of a dialogue) kinds of knowledge. He likens imagination to dreams. He begins, 'Why, you know,' I said, 'that the eyes, when a person directs them towards objects on which the light of day is no longer shining, but the moon and stars only, see dimly, and are nearly blind; they seem to have no clearness of vision in them?' 'Very true'. Then he goes on to say, 'The good is in the intellectual world in relation to mind and the things of mind' (Plato, 1941: 396). Plato seems to be implying that things thought about or from the memory are good and intellectual.

Conversely, both memory and imagination are *image-making* abilities, and their relationships are reinforced by Aristotle who writes that '[t]he thinking faculty thinks of its forms in mental pictures' (Aristotle, 1935: 431b2). A more contemporary view questions the definitive role of images with the intellect: '[r]epresentation of spatial layouts of objects appear to preserve much more abstract and hierarchically organized information than do images or representations of individual objects' (Bjork and Bjork, 1996: 157). The various methods of retrieval and use for diverse cognitive goals account for the flexible way memory, imagination and fantasy are used. New studies have concluded that mental impressions are depictive (like pictures) rather than descriptive representations (tightly linked to and accessed by meaning) (Hinton, 1979; Bjork and Bjork, 1996).

Frances Yates believes it is possible to understand how the connection between memory and intellect became common, since thinking contains the mental impressions from memory and, conversely, memory as a part of learning affects intellectual activity (Yates, 1966). When one is not perceiving, or just knowing, memory comes into play: '[t]he former one claims to perceive and the latter merely to know. But when one has knowledge or sensation without the exercise of these activities, then one remembers' (Aristotle, 1928: *De Memoria* 449b2).

To express the importance of memory in relationship to knowledge, it is necessary to start with a story of how Simonides invented the art of memory (Cicero, 1942). Simonides was called away from a dinner party, and in his absence the roof of the house caved in. His skills in remembering where each individual was sitting facilitated body identification. 'Simonides' invention of the art of memory rested, not only on his discovery of the importance of order for memory, but also on the discovery that the sense of sight is the strongest of all the senses' (Yates, 1966: 4; Cicero, 1942: II.1xxxvi.357).

Although memory involves recalling information, Plato believed that knowledge is not only recollection, but that the soul was elsewhere before it became part of the human body (Plato *Phaedo*, 1953). This universal or human genetic knowledge is reminiscent of Jung's archetypes (Jung, 1983). It is also part of a more contemporary belief that genetically our bodies hold memories (Gregory, 1987). More than a biological explanation, it seems to be a notion that memories are the conduit of knowledge and that somehow these memories are the foundation upon which all knowledge is based (Yates, 1966).

The whole body is involved in the act of memory, since memory, and especially body memory, is *a priori,* constantly at work, never inoperative (Casey, 1987). Philosophers name this body memory ('not memory of the body'), and see it as being '...intrinsic to the body, its own ways of remembering: how we remember in and by and through the body' (Casey, 1987: 147). Body memory can be described as action which was not reflected, not thought about, just enacted as it is 'pre-reflective' and presumed in the experience of humans (Casey, 1987). This interpretation seems to suggest something between subconscious intention and instinct, because often actions do not fit into a mentally remembered place or that which is purely intuitive. Body memory suggests a theory of the body as *habitual* (Merleau-Ponty, 1962). It implies innate past in the body, and that in '...such memory the past is *embodied* in actions' (Casey, 1987: 149). As architects sketch, emotions and actions which are part of the self surface, and become an active part of the sketch in the present (Casey, 1987). It may be that the hand movements involved are neither subconscious nor intuitive. It might be possible then for architects to interject forms (entirely unspecific) that relate to a body memory, in a way that is entirely unknown to their conscious or subconscious memories.

It is important here to interpose the issue that Aristotle finds some differences when comparing memory and reminiscence, or recollection (Aristotle, 1928). *Anamnesis*, recollection or often reminiscence, is similar to the definition of memory as imprint. However, a person with total recall does not necessarily have skills of abstract thought. This might be demonstrated by an *idiot savant*; a person with lower than average intelligence, who can possess incredible capabilities for recall or memorization (Yates, 1966). Recall itself is not the whole of memory, because recollections are recovery of knowledge alone. Recollective knowing, *Mnemosyne*, can be the highest level of knowledge since it is knowledge regained *from within*, from already acquired cognitions. This is not necessarily relearning or just bringing the past to mind but returning to knowledge or, more exactly, memory itself becomes a function of knowledge: '*Mnemosyne*, supernatural power, has been interiorized so as to become in man the very faculty of knowing' (Casey, 1987: 15).

In the writings of Aristotle, the issues of retrieval and memory emerge as the difference between 'passivism' and 'activism'. Passivism depicts that '...in which remembering is reduced to a passive process of registering and storing incoming impressions' (Casey, 1987: 15). This is basically the process of storing information, as epitomized in the wax tablet analogy. Activism on the other hand '...involves the creative transformation of experience rather than its internalized reduplication in images or traces construed as copies' (Casey, 1987: 15). Aristotle's theory permits the capability of the memory or *recollection* to be interpreted through its time in the individual, not as an immediate replica but as a translation dependent upon time elapsed. The traditions of 'activism' might be explained, as in Plato's metaphor of searching for memories, as a process of effective 'working through'.

> Such remembering – such re-viewing and re-valuing – does not require a re-divinization of this elusive power; it is not a question of resurrecting Mnemosyne in person or in name. But it is a matter of re-inspiring respect for what the Greeks called mneme and the Romans memoria. As memor means 'mindful,' so we need to become re-minded, mindful again, mindful of remembering described in its own structure and situated in its own realm – a realm neither mythical nor mechanical but at one with our ongoing existence and experience. (Casey, 1987: 18)

This issue of *working through* has importance for the design process, as the action of recollection combined with knowledge could enhance the interpretive qualities of architectural design and, consequently, sketches. The sketch by Pentti Karoeja (Figure 3.1) displays a page that is covered with three-dimensional sketches studying the Westend Inounnoskirja Day Nursery, Finland Karoeja of Ark-house Architects, in Helsinki, Finland, represents a young and innovative practice building excellent work in steel and wood combinations. These architects have completed projects such as the Helsinki City College of Technology, creating airy open spaces with sensitive proportions. A partner in the firm, Karoeja was the designer for the day nursery. The project presents a playful tenor with colors dancing across patterned façades.

This page shows the sketching and re-sketching of plans and three-dimensional views to interpret the geometric and proportional layout of the building. Each image presents a memory transformed from one image to another. The elements take on similar form since the sketch helps carry the memory between iterations. The images comprise variations on a theme and test the qualities

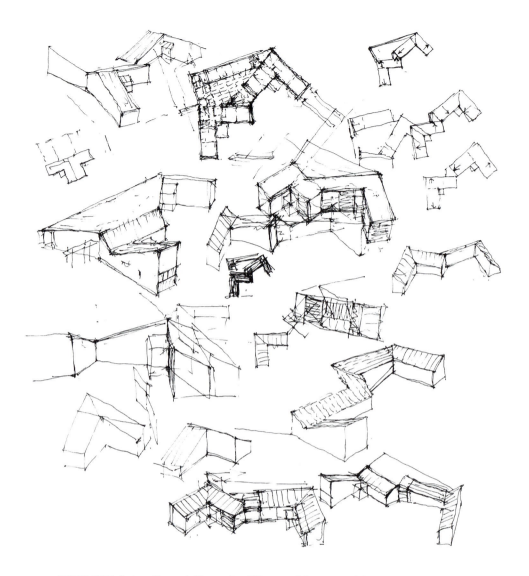

FIGURE 3.1   Pentti Karoeja; Westend Iuonnoskirja Day Nursery.

of visual relationships. The sketches are closely placed and often overlap as Karoeja is drawing quickly. Here it appears he was trying to understand or memorize the building, not create a presentation replication. Each of the sketches has been based on the geometry that is the theme for the project but it seems he was using the plans as memory devices and instilling new compositions and relationships. Obviously remembering the site and program, he was able to move between forms without losing the focus of the project. It appears he was using his active and passive memory to hold and understand the building, and also to learn from and transform the interrelationship of spaces. This expresses part of a process of 'working through' as a mindful memory.

As Simonides invented the art of memory, this analogy can also be seen as the origination of artificial memory. There are two kinds of memory – one natural, the other artificial: '[t]he natural memory is that which is engrafted in our minds, born simultaneously with thought,…[T]he artificial memory is a memory strengthened or confirmed by training' (Yates, 1966: 5).

The study of memory, and Simonides' efforts in practicing to strengthen his ability to remember, prompted exploration of artificial memory. It was a method used by orators walking through a series of rooms to remember certain parts of a speech. In this mnemonic, '[t]he first step was to imprint on the memory a series of *loci* or places,' and thus, artificial memory was established from places and images (Yates, 1966: 3). A *locus* is a place easily grasped by the memory such as a house, arch, or garden. To remember a concept or object, it is possible to place these mental impressions in definite locations (*loci*); these places spark the memory with associations for pre-memorized thoughts. As an example, detective stories often return witnesses to a crime scene in an effort to stimulate their memories for people, details or exact events.

Whereas spaces force remembrance, similarly certain visual settings promote recall of other spatial interactions. It is possible to observe the different roles of location versus object. Cicero wrote '…we may group ideas by means of images and their order by means of localities' (Cicero, 1942: Ixxxviii.359). Because location is spatial, the movement of our bodies through these spaces creates new stimuli to the memory as our position changes. 'For the places are very much like wax tablets or papyrus, the images like the letters, the arrangement and disposition of the images like the script, and the delivery like the reading' (Yates, 1966: 7).

Obviously, movement through rooms is not always practical when trying to remember progression, so *loci* must be manufactured. This is important for architectural sketches, as invention of places and forms in memory affects the creative and imaginative impressions for architecture. Memory can also be visualized in human terms; it might be associated with friends or contrarily with unusual faces (Yates, 1966). Since concentrating on the irregular or abnormal helps an individual stand out in memory, it is also possible to concoct locations and forms for memory; narratives of people and places provide recall. Architects may utilize these modes of recall when sketching to record or design.

Many architects travel accompanied by a sketchbook for visual recording. Several of Antoine Predock's travel sketches provide examples of the relationship between recollection and location. There are several reasons why Predock might want to store images of architecture he has witnessed. If the mind thinks with images as mental impressions, then sketching and thinking simultaneously could help to understand that which is drawn. The intense concentration of drawing can inform knowledge of the subject studied. As Carlo Scarpa wrote that he understood a thing by drawing it, likewise Predock may be using sketches to understand the examples of world architecture he experiences.

In another way, Predock, by drawing, could have been imprinting the perception on a field in his brain, in an attempt to learn it (or encode it). He may have been inspired by the scene and wanted to capture its essence to show colleagues in his office. Figure 3.2 displays a sketch of the Royal Palace in Bangkok. A study of the Bangkok skyline, this sketch relays the distinct and graceful forms of the palace domes. The striking comprehension of the shapes of the domes, along with their color, created an impression Antoine Predock wanted to preserve, possibly a landscape of sinuous form and colors not unlike the desert southwest. This view may have been impossible to explain verbally and required visual clues to recall the momentary experience. As a memory device, the overall impression was more important than the detailing of individual domes. Their juxtaposition and overlap formed a collage that, by sketching the scene, helped to record a spatial relationship so important to the urban context of Bangkok. Predock's use of color, and the loose marks that make up the illustration, display qualities that may represent a method to 'keep' a pleasurable event.

An additional reason to draw an event during travel might be to capture an image to take home to show others. In this way, an experience can be captured for remembrance. Sketches may hold concepts in the form of images for further use in design. Architects often draw architectural space while traveling to collect images as a visual dictionary or thesaurus. A reference point that evokes other mental images could help architects to understand and reuse visual clues for the design process. Throughout the education of architects, students are required to study precedent, which hones these skills of observation and analysis.

Another sketch by Predock presents a contextual impression. Figure 3.3 is a composition from his travels to Chenonceaux, France. Here, shapes on a skyline act as nodes for procession. The building

FIGURE 3.2   Antoine Predock; Royal Palace Bangkok 'An apparition against the sky, played off the insane energy of the Chao Phraya River'.

FIGURE 3.3   Antoine Predock; Chenonceaux, France 'Building as bridge in the fullest sense'.

forms in this sketch appear less important than the view delineating the approach. The sketch reveals a profile of the height of the buildings in comparison to the elevation of the street. Predock may have been exploring the ground to building relationships and these relationships might have provided a visual reference that would assist him when designing similar solid/void juxtaposition. The composition exhibits spatial relationships or proportions that may have aided acts of visualization.

FIGURE 3.4   Steven Holl; Knut Hamsun Museum.

The memory of the scene was supported through the act of sketching and may represent the recording of a spatial precedent for later use.

Memory is often spurred by metaphors; thus *loci* should not be too similar to objects as reminders, because they could be hard to differentiate. In theories of mental impressions, within the study of memory, there are two kinds of these forms: one for 'things' and the other for 'words' (Cicero, 1942). 'Things' are thus the subject matter of the speech; 'words' are the language in which that subject matter is clothed' (Yates, 1966: 8–9). It is much easier to find an object or picture that reminds one of a thing. It is possible that a word is more specific causing abstract associations to be limited. The question arises as to whether remembering the object which gives recall for the specific word is as difficult as remembering the word itself.

In the same vein, metaphors can become too confusing, as the complex mental impressions, which lead to allusion, are more difficult to remember than the original concept or object itself. The step between the postulate and the representative metaphor is often too distant and can get lost in new analogies. These mental impressions might be confusing, '[b]ecause metaphors represent a thing less accurately than the description of the actual thing itself' (Yates, 1966: 65). Although the actual reminders give more exact information about the thing itself, metaphors (*metaphoria*) '…move the soul more and therefore better help the memory' (Yates, 1966: 65).

Architects may utilize words, in addition to images, to further define objects or events. If a drawing seems incomplete, and they fear it will be forgotten, or misunderstood, architects can clarify with words. As an example, in Figure 3.4 Steven Holl uses words to provide information impossible to relay in a quick sketch, such as color or materials. His Knut Hamsun Museum in Hamarøy,

Norway, is a metaphor for the dark wood Nordic churches of the area. The building's concept 'building as body,' expresses this concern with orifices and protrusions emulating a human body.

In this sketch, Holl employs words to elaborate on his visual notes. This notation is adjacent to and almost overlapping a plan and elevation sketches for the Knut Hamsun Center. Although exhibiting a small hillside, Holl writes a reminder along side the building elevation – 'windows frame mountain views'. This note acts as a memory device to hold critical information. Although it is unlikely this information would be forgotten, the verbiage helps to explain his thinking during the process. The limitations of the sketch prevent him from drawing the mountain view, or even the image of the mountain, but the note helps remind him of the issues important in the siting of this building.

Other notes assist in defining and remembering the process as 'isolated balconies' and 'one wooden bench'. Limitations of the sketch may keep the bench form from being recognized. In a plan drawing, and certainly in a sketch, a bench may be appropriately portrayed as four lines that make a rectangle. Without adequate notation the lines could represent steps, or a table, for example. The message that says 'isolated balconies' helps clarify a function that may be obvious but may also have been included to act as a reminder. The words may have also reinforced a design decision.

On the top right of the sketch, Holl has made a legend to indicate materials. The sod roof is obvious but the specifications for steel and wood are less easy to represent in a plan and needed to be clarified. The materials chosen for this project might not be recognized without the use of words, since the sketches provide visual impressions but cannot furnish specifics. Along with the inherent incompleteness of words and sketches, the function of the sketch in recording also acts as a notebook to record the process and the decisions to be remembered throughout the process.

Similarly, in a sketch by Renzo Piano (Figure 3.5) words assist the architect's ability to remember and analyze. The Renzo Piano Building Workshop is located in Genoa, Italy, the place of his birth. Beginning his architectural career using structure as a way to articulate his buildings, his style was labeled High Tech. Currently employing architectural character based on technological forms, he experiments with materials with 'elegantly expressed structure'. Honored with the 1998 Pritzker Architecture Prize, Renzo Piano's buildings blur the boundaries between technology and art. Several of his most celebrated projects include the Redevelopment of the Genoa Old Harbour, the Zentrum Paul Klee Museum in Bern, the Jean-Marie Tjibaou Cultural Center in Noumea, New Caledonia and most recently the Shard London Bridge Skyscraper.

This sketch appears to be a design analysis for the London Bridge Tower. The drawings on the page support the analytical thinking that uses images to initiate design decisions, since the images create questions that need appropriate solutions. The sketch exhibits a diagrammatic elevation/ section of the tower. Here, Piano employs a fluid green felt pen to outline the form with surprisingly straight lines. Piano's control of the medium by using swift strokes may account for the very straight lines. Although the marks are made with a confident hand that presumes a predetermined form, he was using this sketch to ponder. Important intersections (or areas of concern) have received highlights in red colored pencil. In several areas dots can be seen as places where the pen rested on the paper, possibly a moment for Piano to collect his thoughts.

As with any opportunity for analysis, this sketch seems to provide Piano with a personal dialogue. He writes notes concerning issues he wishes to remember and, also, provides emphasis by using exclamation marks in an effort to reinforce intentions. Analysis involves isolating portions for specific study and this can be viewed distinctly in the red 'hot' spots of activity. Either a typical convention of drawing or a need to recall relationships, he draws arrows between the words and the corresponding image. The words record locations of significant building elements and methods of treatment. Piano's use of words may act, or assist, the act of articulating concepts he wanted to imprint on his mind. Not surprisingly the rest of the tower remains relatively vague and diagrammatic. This example reflects the limitations of quick sketches; they may provide impressions but cannot furnish specifics.

Remembering and recording decisions can be a function of sketches for architects. A sketch by Erich Mendelsohn (Figure 3.6) demonstrates this function well. Erich Mendelsohn began his architectural career in Germany in the 1920s and 1930s with projects such as the Albert Einstein

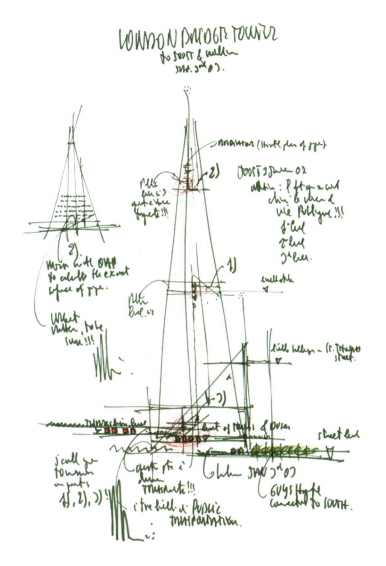

FIGURE 3.5   Renzo Piano's sketch, September 2003 — hand drawing on paper showing the project of the London Bridge Tower.

Observatory in Potsdam. Once associated with the Futurist Movement, he spoke about his work in terms of *Dynamism* that was manifest in expressionistic and individual design. His other projects in Germany include the Schocken Department Stores and Columbus-Haus in Potsdammer Platz, Berlin. In the years before World War II he emigrated to Israel, then England and eventually to the United States. He settled in California, teaching and lecturing along with designing community and religious buildings, such as the Hebrew University in Jerusalem.

This project, the Library and Office Building for Salmon Schocken in Jerusalem, consists of several hard-edged drawings of elevations and freehand perspectives. The ruled drawings show façades with extensive ground to roof windows. In this example, Mendelsohn was using the drawings and sketches for evaluation and decision-making. On two of the most dominant elevations, he has drawn large x's across the windows. The x's act as a decision he was concerned would be forgotten. The marks may have provided definitive elimination as not to be confused with chosen compositions.

FIGURE 3.6   Erich Mendelsohn; Library and Office Building of Salman Schocken, Jerusalem, perspectives and elevation.

This confirmation may have been for his personal benefit or to ensure that others in his office understood his intentions. The action (x's) could also represent a physical act that, by doing, made the decision more conclusive. A diagonal line can be seen on the center elevation, which may not have been sufficiently bold. In this condition, the heavier crosses reinforced the decision.

Three perspective sketches to the right of the page show alternatives with smaller punched windows. These sketches were completed after the ruled elevations because the lower one overlaps an elevation. This overlapping shows a disregard for the earlier version by partially obliterating the form. The top of the page has a large X, which has been circled. Possibly rejecting the drawings and then returning to them, Mendelsohn may have needed to iterate the validity of the new decision. The middle sketch on the right is accented by a check, which may also indicate a positive assessment. The perspective on the lower right has been 'finished' with an arc, possibly providing a background horizon. It is also possible that seeing the completed illusion may have helped Mendelsohn arrive at the most adequate solution, thus the arc may have functioned as a variation on a circle – to emphasize a positive solution.

It appears Mendelsohn was using the sketches to remember important decisions and the evaluation of a design element. It is unknown whether he made those decisions immediately after drawing the image, or at a later date. If he was critiquing his sketches while they were being drawn, this might indicate that he used the sketches primarily to test his designs. Although this process of viewing thoughts visually can represent a mode of critique, it is only one of a variety of reasons architects use sketches, and it would be unusual if Mendelsohn saw this as their only function. But the act of crossing out images which are no longer useful, or appropriate, is a method to preserve a decision, as a memory device. Several hundred years earlier Borromini (Figure 2.4) had used a similar technique to record decisions in a process, and the visual qualities of the image imprint the conclusion. The mode of resemblance might be at issue here.

Resemblance is an 'indication' that provokes a memory. 'Indication', as the relationship between reminder and remindand, is a sign that evokes an action by signaling its actual or possible presence. '[A] thing is only properly an indication if and where it in fact serves to indicate something *to some thinking being*' (Casey, 1987: 96). Here Edward Casey emphasizes the important tie in memory to architectural representation as a spatial and imaging discipline.

In the mental activity of imaging for design, recollections spark association through similarity or dissimilarity (Aristotle, 1928; Hume, 1978). This most often happens with memory, because the mind (as in reminiscence) wanders when not immediately stimulated. It is possible to conclude thinking about something very different from where one began because of a train of associations. This connection of 'free associations' constitutes the search for abstract concepts and form in the design process. Architects depend on memory and imagination to mingle and furnish new interpretations.

Association is a quality seen in many architectural sketches. Often the images made by the hand spark a series of similar or associative thoughts. These sketches may act as variations on a theme where one image is transformed into a like image – as the different is infused into the familiar. One sketch may then start a reaction that the architect cannot control as memory and association flow. On a page of sketches by Michael Rotondi (Figure 3.7) it is possible to view what may be a series of associative images. It appears that the architect's memory combined with imagination creates a thoughtful opportunity for idea generation. Michael Rotondi was a co-founding partner of the practice Morphosis. In 1991, as principal, he opened RoTo Architects. Based in Los Angeles, Rotundi has completed such projects as UCSD Joan and Irwin Jacobs Center for the La Jolla Playhouse, the Sinte Gleska University in South Dakota (buildings and master plan), and numerous private residences. He has received many American Institute of Architects awards and views his practice as a teaching lab for young graduates of architecture schools.

This page is a whimsical flow of three-dimensional, and plan, forms. Appearing haphazard the sketches are instead meaningful and intentional techniques he uses for inspiration. Rotondi discusses his use of sketches as *idea-gram*; they give him an opportunity to think through conceptual beginnings while drawing. He writes: 'drawing is the way I think visually – outside my head, and while I am drawing by hand it gives me time to think as well as reach higher states of concentration – fun and meditational.'[1]

On this page, the three-dimensional shapes morph easily into plans or diagrams. To the left can be viewed blimp-like three-dimensional forms. The lines carry to the center with a landscape and contained diagram that may pertain to orientation. The right side of the sketch displays watercolor forms, and on the lower right a scale for measurement or music. The way one line begins as a figure and ends in a different context suggests that the sketches were employed to connect disparate thoughts that may begin with one idea and end with another. If this were true, the changing context from one side of the page to the other presents a view of the process. The remarkable creativity that stems from the association of lines, in juxtaposition to each other, reveals an active mind.

---

[1] From a written statement by Michael Rotondi when asked about his use of sketches.

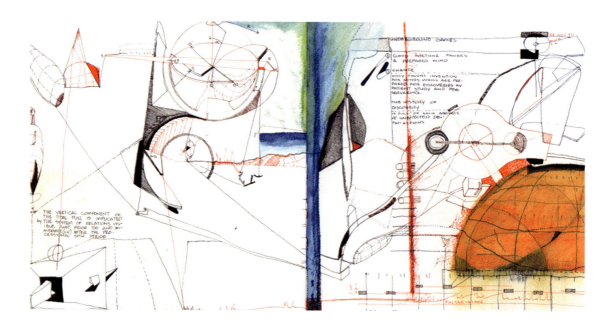

FIGURE 3.7   Michael Rotondi; idea-gram. 'Drawing an idea-gram is conducive to the speed of my generative thinking. It's the right speed.'

Interjected into the images are philosophical writings that may frame the exploration. Although seemingly arbitrary, the images contain a theme and volume relationship to suggest Rotondi's memory connects the forms to investigate new approaches to a specific destination. It is suspected that he does not know where the exercise will lead him but trusts the process of association.

In a sketch by Michelangelo (Figure 3.8) it is possible to view an additional example of associative memory. This page has been covered with various versions of molding profiles. These profiles exhibit the depth and section shape of carving at the base of columns. The fact that Michelangelo was concerned with the exaggeration and manipulation of column bases references his concern for the Mannerist development as an evolution from Renaissance ideals. Michelangelo, a Renaissance architect, was also a painter and sculptor.

His adherence to *designo*, the Renaissance concept of idea, is evident in this sketch. The molding profiles are juxtaposed with sketches of faces, which may be a factor of a need by Michelangelo to draw on every piece of paper at hand. Thus it may have been purely accidental that they appear on the same page, they may also represent a conscious, or subconscious, egalitarian treatment of the subjects in his mind. Each was considered an opportunity for exploration with ink or graphite, whether a human or stone column base. Michelangelo also may have comprehended a relationship between the two; the molding profiles caricaturing human faces. The profile on the upper right corner of the page seems to include an eye. Some of the profiles are drawn to appear much like human profiles, even to the point of curling the upper lip down (as in the profile on the upper left), a detail not practical for a column base in stone. The association between the profiles and heads may have been logical for him.

Comparatively, the volume of faces and molding profiles, both subjects which Michelangelo worked in stone, may have developed a strong relationship in his mind. The faces have been sketched with graphite while the profiles were drawn in brown or sepia ink. It is impossible to know which were drawn first, since the faces fit into the empty center of the page. A faint mustached face, in graphite, on the lower left, suggests the ink was the later medium. In which case, the faces may have influenced the form of the profiles. The speculation that the relationships between the

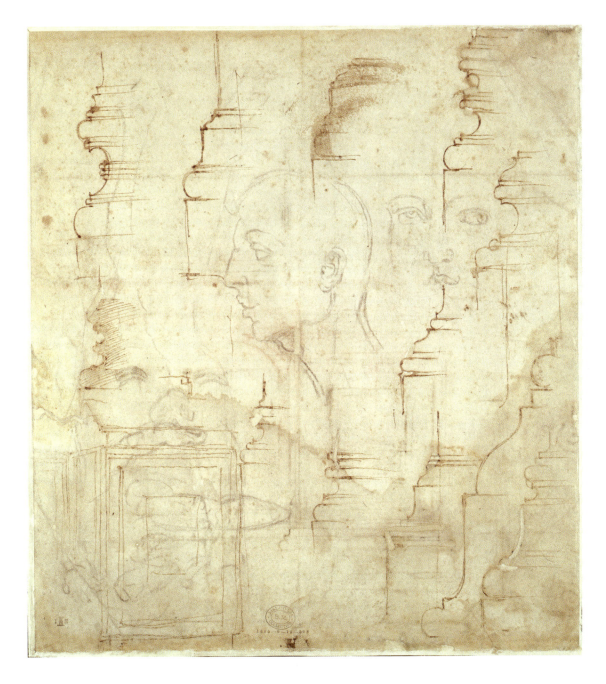

FIGURE 3.8   Michelangelo Buonarroti (1475–1564); Sketches of columns and faces
(pen, pencil and ink on paper).

forms may have been subconscious, questions the memory of the body, as eyes and hands may act independently of the conscious mind. It might be easy to understand the use of recall and association when studying memory of events and written language; it is less so when discussing *mneme* or enacted body memory.

The idea of 'time elapsed' can also suggest the active 'working through' of a design. As remnants of thinking or working on a design, sketches are often vague, redrawn, and drawn over (with

55

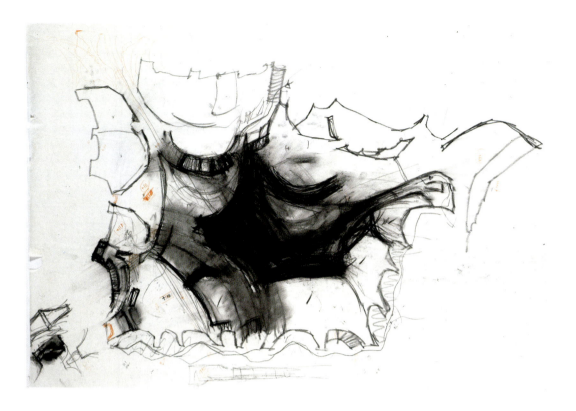

FIGURE 3.9   Reima Peitilä; Kaleva Church, Tampere.

overlapping lines – lines drawn on top of lines) in a pondering manner. Contrarily, sketches can be fast flowing lines that might be racing to capture an escaping thought. As *mneme* they are 'mindful or reminded' in whatever form they take because the notion of time reveals memories and the interpretation which transforms them. Translation is also difficult to recognize, since these sketches become intensely personal.

A sketch by Reima Pietilä (Figure 3.9) for the Kaleva Church, Tampere, Finland, reveals several elusive qualities of *mneme*. This sketch of a building plan shows a thought process that embodies a concept of time. The sketch was completed in three media, as if each medium fulfilled a distinct purpose. The layout or outline has been drawn in graphite and the center section has been rendered in a soft medium such as charcoal. The erasures and smears reflect a manner of evaluation, a 'working through' the process. Either Peitilä was unconcerned that the erasures were not complete, or with his excitement to view the form emerging on the page, he 'erased' with his fingers.

The lines in pencil seem to be fast and sketchy, whereas the lines in charcoal are bold and expressive, evoking the volume of the space. These heavy lines have been drawn quickly as he *poches* the thickness of the walls. The smeared and 'gestural' marks suggest an amount of time, as if he was working and reworking the plan over a period of time. It appears he was afraid to move to another sheet of paper in fear of losing a sequence of thought, as he was continually reinforcing the dark lines to make visual corrections. Immersed in the action of the sketch, small dots of charcoal appear across the page, where Peitilä rested his charcoal covered fingers. This sketch reveals a thinking process where it is possible to view the beginning, and comprehend the labor, of the development.

For architectural design, and especially sketching as a manifestation of the process, the experience of the past had a great influence on the present, especially concerning interpretation of its form. The importance of location for a spatial discipline such as architecture, as well as recollective knowing, the use of analogies, and metaphors, is revealed in sketches by architects. Imagination, the topic of the following discussion, speaks of the future rather than the past. The two are inherently connected, since the imagination makes use of the mental impressions of memory. This active memory has the ability to make forms from memory, in combination and interpretation, to provide entirely new compositions. Distinctly different from 'recall', the imagination working on memory expands this faculty of knowing.

IMAGINATION

The 'image' of imagination is difficult to define because all humans experience imagination and know how mental impressions occur in the mind, but the ability to describe these experiences is elusive. A definition of imagination reflects the study of perception, as the mental impressions of perception are often worked on by imagination. Imagination is frequently used to envisage objects which are absent from view, to change or interpret that which can be observed, or to recognize and reuse items which are known (Warnock, 1976). 'One might add that in this capacity it [imagination] is often defined as a faculty for finding analogies' (Brann, 1991: 23). The element most characteristic of imagination is that it involves change and interpretation of what can be observed.

It is surprising how often and easily humans use aspects of imagination. Edward Casey describes two characteristics of imagining: that imagination is easy to engage, and that we can imagine *whatever* and *however* we would like (Casey, 1976). The ability to so easily use a function of the mind without obvious effort has fascinated philosophers through history in their effort to describe or define imagination.

Plato explains that the soul is like the eye, but when the eye is not perceiving; imagination and thinking are opinion only and are erratic (Plato, 1941). In comparison, philosophers from Aristotle to Immanuel Kant view imagination less harshly, and assign it a mediating state (Casey, 1976). David Hume felt that the role of imagination was that of mediation between impressions and aspects of memory or judgment:

> *Those perceptions which enter with most force and violence we may name* impressions; *and under this name I comprehend all our sensations, passions and emotions, as they make their first appearance in the soul. By* ideas *I mean the faint images of these in thinking and reasoning. (Hume, 1978: 1)*

Hume defined 'ideas' as different from perceptions, viewing them as the leftover essence of perception that is used for thinking and reasoning. In this manner, perceptions are connected to cognitive activity. He viewed the force of memory and perceptions, in contrast to the subtle and vague workings of the imagination on these perceptions. Hume described imagination as having the liberty '...to transpose and change its ideas'. In this way, he was regarding imagination as a recombination of sense memory, since this connection creates a bond between 'ideas' as associations (Hume, 1978).

A sketch that is both ruled and freehand, for example the sketch by the Italian designer Carlo Scarpa (Figure 3.10), demonstrates the way imagination works on images to transform concepts. This sketch reveals a thinking process as Scarpa alters and erases drawn images to test and visualize. Carlo Scarpa was born in Venice in 1906. He studied at the Architectural Institute of Venice University where he later became a Professor and Director. Known for his remarkably sensitive manipulation of materials and techniques, his work displays not only craftsmanship, but a unique combination, juxtaposition, and balance of materials. His most celebrated commissions include the Canova Plaster Cast Gallery in Possagno; the Castelvecchio Museum in Verona, begun in 1956;

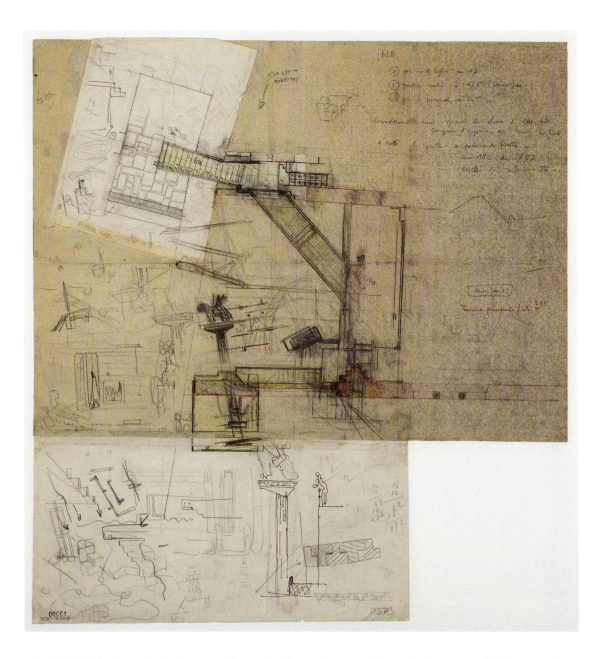

FIGURE 3.10   Carlo Scarpa; Pianta dell'area di esposizione della statua di Cangrande;
studi per il supporto della statua esquestre in un'ipotesi a colonne. (Location of the
Langrande statue; studies for the support of the equestrian statue in conceptual
relationship to the columns.)

the Olivetti Showroom in Piazza S. Marco, Venice; and the Brion Tomb in San Vito d'Altivole.
His skills in uniting memory with contemporary proportions show in his sketches.

As a professor of drawing, Scarpa extensively utilized sketches, combined with drawing, as a
medium for design. One interesting technique was to sketch on top, and in the margins, of ruled

drawings using various methods of erasure. He often 'erased' by using gesso to block out certain areas, providing an opportunity to redraw, or pasted additional sheets to the one of immediate interest. It is possible that Scarpa would draw a design proposal and then critique the solution employing other images. It is also conceivable that once he perceived the solution it sparked new ideas and refinement. In either case, he used the drawings as references for the continuation of his design process, possibly a reason that he did not move to a separate, clean sheet. The result became a layering of gesso, graphite, erasures, colored pencils and pasted paper appliqué. This result also evidenced the drawing as a memory device, since he could view, remember and manipulate the images once they appeared on the paper. This working through the design helped him envision the three-dimensional structure, and may have acted as the medium for his imagination.

Figure 3.10 demonstrates several of these techniques by Scarpa. This sketch is a study for the placement of the Cangrande statue in the Castelvecchio Museum, Verona, Italy. The sheet has been patched and extended with additional pieces of paper. In the center is placed a drafted plan of the area with pathways and stairs. The margins are filled with small details, perspectives and notes. The pieces of paper added on the top right appear to be covering a former solution and present the opportunity to try an alternative, with the ability to refer to the original spatial relationships. Applying onto the original may have saved time, but it also meant that Scarpa could view the history of his design thinking. Had he started over, the past investigations would have been lost.

This page shows how he participated physically with the drawings, emphasizing with colored pencil and heavier lines. This technique was most likely a way to differentiate, or track, the alterations and decisions. The page of sketches reveals the elapsed time in the process and how memory is altered by imagination. It also explains much of Scarpa's use of imagination; he moves easily between construction details, diagrams, elevations, and perspectives visualizing the various aspects of the sculpture and the architecture so vital to its display. Here, memory and perceptions are transformed by the imagination, as the sketch becomes the process and medium for thinking dependent upon reference.

Similar to Hume, Kant finds an interdependence between intellect and perception in imagination as synthesis (Warnock, 1976). The productive type has a constructive function more consistent with conceptual thinking. With the synthesis of imagination, neither perception or thinking alone can be creative.

> *We are now in a position to see that (both for Hume and Kant) it is the* representational *power of the imagination, its power, that is, actually to form images, ideas or likenesses in mind which is supposed to contribute to our awareness of the world… Kant describes the imagination as a mysterious faculty which enables us to go beyond the immediate object of sense, and recognize it as a member of a kind of objects, and as a faculty which does this by means of actual images or representations which we can form for ourselves in our minds. (Warnock, 1976: 33)*

The new mental impression cannot be radically new, because the imagination is a synthesis of memory and perception, and all that can be originated is dependent on these (Casey, 1976). To make a new combination, such as a unicorn, the mind must remember a horse and a horn. In a similar situation, science fiction stories contain enough of the present, in their view of the future, to be believable to personal experience. Consequently, architects using sketches for conceptual inspiration will draw what they know in an attempt to, through associations of images, find new combinations. The imagination '…invents a concept, or calls one up, to fit the visible or audible form before it' (Warnock, 1976: 49). In this way imagination finds a certain shape or form – an order out of chaos. The imagination's dependence upon both memory and perception is expressed here because the architect in the present is both remembering (in a *mnemosyne* sense) and anticipating the future.

There are several characteristics of the imagination that assist in understanding its activities. The first are *spontaneity* and *controlledness* (Casey, 1976). Humans can control imaginings by simply deciding to. The capability of conjuring a mental impression is contrasted, or complemented, by the chance of something spontaneous happening, such as the mind leaping to a different form.

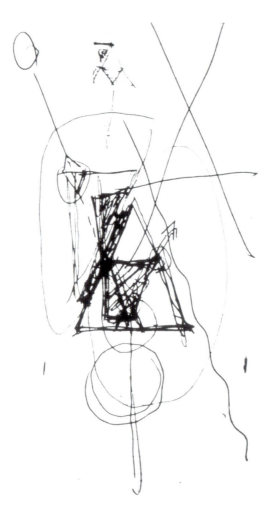

FIGURE 3.11   I.M. Pei; East Wing of the National Gallery of Art, Washington, D.C.

This expresses an associative, spontaneous image in the form of a mental impression, but the spontaneous phenomenon can initiate itself rather than being initiated.

Imagination has additional traits, those of *self-containedness* and *self-evidence*. The imaginer's desire determines the range of possible imaginings, and this product will have features that the imaginative activity imposes on it. The imagination is self-evident in that all information appears at once, and issues of inconsistency are unimportant.

A sketch for the East Wing of the National Gallery in Washington, D.C. by Ieoh Ming Pei (Figure 3.11) contains qualities of self-containedness. Born in China, I.M. Pei has designed such buildings as the pyramid for the Louvre in Paris; the Bank of China in Hong Kong; the Javits Convention Center in New York; and the Rock and Roll Hall of Fame in Cleveland. Pei has been continually honored for his steel, glass and concrete modern buildings that make use of simple geometric shapes. His awards include the 1979 American Institute of Architects Gold Medal and he was recipient of the 1983 Pritzker Architecture prize.

On this page it is possible to view a brief but expressive sketch plan for the museum. It appears Pei was searching for geometric relationships between the triangle buildings and the features on the site. This may be evident in the wavy line that runs down the right side of the building forms. The upper left shows a study of the corner of the building. This emphasis on 'corner' may have been a reminder about a feature on the site. The space between the shapes has been more heavily articulated to suggest this interstitial space was of primary concern in his visual dialogue. This might be a very early exploration, since the form appears to be a reversal of the final constructed building. The large X to the upper right of the page may be a diagram, or *parti*, showing the basic relationships of the geometries.

The sketch, beautiful in its precision uses elements such as circles to accent part of the building that needed attention. Although studying several aspects of the building in plan, this sketch page is limited to Pei's exploration of a specific element, as his thoughts are intent on resolving one aspect of the project. The sketch was not distracted by peripheral objects but concentrates on momentary concerns and thus displays a self-containedness of the imagination.

The sketch also speaks of a self-evidence, because the images are not grounded and are disparate elements reflecting the focus of his momentary attention. They may not appear all at once but the pieces are viewed as an entirety even though they are unfinished fragments. Although more ambiguous and implied, scale and consistency are unimportant to evaluate the concept, as are qualities of spontaneity and controlledness. The images are controlled by their topic but do not rule out the possibility of interjecting the new.

Two additional aspects of imagination that most influence architectural sketches are *indeterminacy* and *pure possibility*. Indeterminacy describes how it is difficult to determine exactly where imagined objects begin or end or precisely where they are located. Imagination does not necessarily follow rules of perspective, and the scene's edges might disappear or the scene itself might quickly change location. In this way, anything imagined has qualities of being possible. Pure possibility can be seen as '…the "purity" of imaginative possibilities [that] lies precisely in their independence of the mutually exclusive alternatives of reality and unreality' (Casey, 1976: 113). This aspect of imagination makes anything hypothetical and all things possible.

The *possibilizing* activity allows the artist a wide field of play, since the creativity of imagination is further distinguished by its virtual autonomy. Freudian psychoanalysis, stressing pure possibility, introduces free associations which include memories, dreams, daydreams, imaginings and fantasies (Casey, 1976). Which brings this discussion to Carl Jung and his three forms of fantasy or imagination: voluntary, passive and active (Jung, 1953, 1979).

For Jung, passive imagination is the uncontrollable, where one is overwhelmed by the upsurge of one's own fantasies. This seems very similar to the un-containing qualities of pure possibility. Active imagination involves a positive participation of consciousness, as the conscious self enters into its own activity (Jung, 1953, 1979). Contrarily, the passive imagination seems curious, for the activity of suppressing the conscious level of the mind indicates the lack of intentionality. Some architects, when searching for inspiration in a design process, sketch while accompanied by a distraction, such as television or music. This might be a method to externally stimulate the subconscious so as to allow the mind to have passive participation with the imagination and thus trust intuition.

Intentionality can be seen as the ordering principle for imagination. Before one calls up a mental impression, a decision must be made to do so, and the form envisaged is created by one's choice. Even if the mind free associates and lets unusual possibilities flow, one is intentionally choosing to allow them. As in reminiscing, humans control to some extent whether or not they engage in free associations or change to another subject. These seem to exhibit acts of possibilizing which allow a creative solution of the future because all three functions are an indication of that which may have never existed. Although they are contingent upon memory to determine these various new conclusions, they are both intentional and creative.

It is timely to turn to a few examples that may illustrate the role of imagination for architects when sketching. An architectural sketch by Mayumi Miyawaki (Figure 3.12) is a design sketch for the Yokoo Residence (Akahira, 1982). Miyawaki was a founding member of the group *Architext*. Publishing their work in a series of monographs, this group of five Japanese architects was devoted to innovative and experimental architecture. Designing the Izushi Junior High School along with many residences, Miyawaki combined traditional elements with modern attributes.

FIGURE 3.12   Mayumi Miyawaki; Sketch of Yokoo Residence, 1979.

This sketch seems to be an increasingly more detailed series of exterior massing forms culminations with two plans. The volume drawings have a similarity of theme – a self-containedness. As in play, the shape is drawn repeatedly, with changes becoming more and more specific. Miyawaki emphasizes this connection by stating that certain drawings became stepping stones for the rest. Their associative qualities are evident in their subtle evolution, and the sketches reveal a controlledness in intention. The specific site and program guide this project, even to a note written on the sketch: 'low cost'. Miyawaki writes on this drawing about his intentions: '[h]owever, an image of "primary box" which just fits the environment was already in my mind then.' This strict adherence to the program is contrasted by quick and incomplete sketches, which might indicate this architect's ability to allow spontaneity within the framework. Miyawaki's imagination combines program memories with the possibilities of form.

A sketch by Cesar Pelli (Figure 3.13) provides insight into the elements of imagination. Pelli Clarke Pelli Architects, once Cesar Pelli & Associates, is located in Connecticut. An immigrant

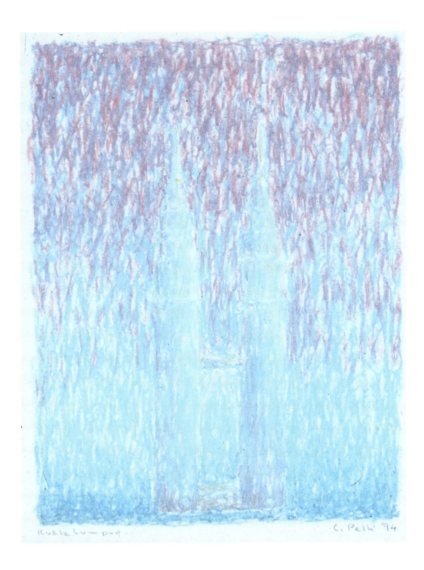

FIGURE 3.13   Cesar Pelli; Petronas Towers.

from Argentina, Cesar Pelli has built an incredible number of sophisticated projects throughout the world. The firm has received over 40 American Institute of Architects awards including the 1995 Gold Medal. Responding to the particularities of site and program rather than maintaining a distinctive 'style', Pelli and partners have completed such diverse projects as the Aronoff Center for the Arts, the Beijing World Financial Center, Rice University Herring Hall, Yale University Malone Engineering Center and the celebrated Petronas Twin Towers in Kuala Lumpur.

This design sketch of the towers captures emotional and metaphorical dimensions of an architect's imagination. Pelli writes: '[I] did several oil pastel drawings of the Petronas Towers trying to imagine how they would react to the changing light and weather of Kuala Lumpur.'[2] This sketch demonstrates a soft atmospheric allusion of the twin towers almost obscured by the use of pastels. The towers have been drawn in blue and, to blend the building with the background, Pelli has chosen the same hue of blue. The towers present little detail and act as an overall impression, not

---

[2] From a statement by Cesar Pelli when asked about how he uses sketches.

unlike a dream or fleeting impression. The vagueness allows allusion in stark contrast to an illusion of a perspective intended for a realistic experience and instead this sketch epitomizes an emotional experience. Not necessarily meant to present information such as materiality, Pelli's sketch conveys an impression of an imagined future. Pelli expresses this well when he writes:

> *In this particular drawing, I was thinking of the very heavy, humid haze that sometimes hangs on Kuala Lumpur like a veil. I was trying to capture how the forms of the Towers would blend with the sky. Now that the towers are built, this condition does occur occasionally, although not as often as I imagined, and it is best perceived at a good distance where there is some depth of atmosphere between the observer and the Towers. When seen like that they are a very poetical image.*[3]

The indeterminacy of the architectural sketch makes it difficult to specifically locate objects, and thus provides fertile ground for the imagination. Pelli's sketch, in light of his verbiage, shows an undefined combination of forms, where the background is somewhat indistinguishable from the foreground. The loose and fluid lines overlap and give a general haze to the whole drawing – merging the building with its surroundings. This vagueness provides the viewer with the ability to project onto the drawing, and thus project impressions from the ambiguity. The materials and functions of form stimulate multiple possibilities, as the observer is given a general feeling rather than the shape of a specific building.

The synthesis of sensory and mental faculties, which play with or transform impressions into concepts, has a dimension of creation which begins to consider pure possibility. Especially in the late Middle Ages and the Renaissance, imagination took on a new autonomous quality linked to artists and the madness of inspiration, not understood by the average person. Although fantasy and imagination are often interchangeable, the word *fantasy* evokes the image of that which has never been seen (unlike imagination which could be 'to bring a memory image to mind'). This discussion must turn to the future of fantasy.

FANTASY

Although imagination and fantasy are virtually synonymous, fantasy includes an additional dimension of creativity, illusion, or hallucination. Thinkers throughout history, and especially during the Renaissance, have speculated about the mind's ability to create. Creative inspiration may be credited to an expanded associative capacity of certain individuals or it may be attributed to magic or divine intervention. Another word, *fancy*, which has a similar meaning, describes a fantastic or whimsical nature or an impression or fantastic invention created by the mind. This investigation will shed light on the importance of creative imagination in the act of architectural sketching.

If fantasy constitutes envisioning the unknown, then the significance of an architectural sketch that epitomizes the unknown becomes evident. Although architectural sketches are used in many ways, one important aspect involves what they reveal about the yet unseen architecture. Rudolf and Margot Wittkower write in their book *Born Under Saturn* that in the history of the western world, only twice were artists elevated from craftsmen to inspired artists: in fourth-century Greece and in fifteenth-century Italy (1963). In this time of raised consciousness pertaining to artists in society, the divine inspiration they seemed to possess was not limited to specific media. The artist was likened, for example, to the poet who was felt to embody creative imagination, and all the arts were entwined in a concept of design (Gordon, 1975).

---

[3] From a statement by Cesar Pelli when asked about his thinking while completing this sketch.

Fantasia may mean creative imagination, but this was not originally the case (Summers, 1981). When the word *phantasia* first appeared in western literature, it meant the appearance or the reflection of a thing, and was a metaphor of the mind as a mirror. With fantasy and imagination having similar meaning, the nearest Greek equivalent to imagination comes from '"to be like" or "capable of being compared"' (Bundy, 1927: 11). The reflection, then, is a copy or imitation, although the likeness need not be a replica. David Summers writes that *phantasia* and a higher reality are linked by divination, writing of the two sides of fantasy '…one that reflects the world of sense, and another, allied with memory, that presents the reflected image to the higher faculties of the soul.' He continues by saying that this 'image' has been in 'combinatory fantasy to make "what had never been seen"' (1981, 108).

It was the talent of the artist to make things that had never been seen before. The layman, in awe of the artist able to create totally bizarre illusions, gave the artist a reputation as a thaumaturgist (Summers, 1981). The myth was perpetuated by the artists themselves and those who wrote about them. Giorgio Vasari, for example, in his book on the lives of Renaissance artists, plays on the quirks and chance beginnings which gave these artists mythical proportions, accentuating the artists' eccentric behavior, genius, madness, and melancholy.

Artists and architects were seen as having special abilities sanctioned by a supreme being. As an example, it was reported by Vasari that the artist Fra Angelico did not retouch his paintings after they were finished because God's will was done through the artist's hand (1946). Kris and Kurz provide another example from an eleventh-century Chinese painter who advised artists to look to a broken wall as inspiration for landscape painting. 'For them, he said, you can let your brush follow the play of your imagination, and the result will be heavenly and not human' (1979: 47). Though from different periods and different continents, these two views hold artists' inspiration to be divine. The artist was described as being possessed or as having 'poetic madness' (*mania* and *techne*) (Barasch, 1985).

The Renaissance viewed artists, along with poets, in the 'circle of inspired creators' (Wittkower and Wittkower, 1963: 98). Their concept of the *divino artista,* or divine artist, had two meanings, which divided the artist from laymen. Wittkower states, '[i]t was not only derived from Plato's theory of poetical enthusiasm but also from the medieval idea of God the Father as artist: as architect of the universe' (1963: 98). The artist, able to recognize divine beauty, was driven to divine madness and, consequently, these artists were forgiven eccentric behavior, distinctive of their creative imaginations.

There are many examples of writers of the Renaissance who expound on the connection between fantasy and madness. One is Dante Alighieri who was a writer with incredible visual qualities, he '…affirms more powerfully than anyone before him − both in theory and creative accomplishment − that fantasy was much greater than the sum of its parts…he speaks of fantasy (or imagination) as a force initiated by divine grace which, like the intellect it serves, is able to approach the threshold of the vision of light itself' (Summers, 81: 119). Dante was unwilling to view imagination as images worked on by our minds, as a sole definition. He was alluding to an intuitive God-given talent that enters a realm beyond: of magic, divination or *invenzione*.

David Summers, in trying to demarcate the boundaries of *fantasia* as used by Michelangelo, writes '…*fantasia* is closest in meaning to *invenzione*' (1981: 103). A term used extensively in the Renaissance, *invenzione*, resembles the modern meaning to invent: to originate as a product of one's own device, or to make up or fabricate. The word *invenzione* is interesting in the way it became connected with the arts. 'Invention' originated as a technical term from rhetoric. It was primary in the five-part division of rhetoric, and consisted of '…the finding out or selection of topics to be treated, or arguments to be used' (Gordon, 1975: 93). During the Renaissance period, it was used commonly in poetic theory, with a definition similar to that held in rhetoric; 'invention' now holds a creative connotation.

Invention is literally the finding of the subject of the poem. Invention is also equated with the fable or fiction of the poem…The 'invention' is the fable itself and the theme it carries. It is close to the words 'argument' and 'device' and should be taken with them. When the fable is stated as a narrative it is the 'argument', the plot-line; but argument can also mean the subject, the theme illustrated by the fable. 'Device' means plot-line, fable or narrative. 'Invention' is the most inclusive term. (Gordon, 1975: 82)

This explanation is interesting for architecture, since the invention suggests an architectural 'concept'. Invention as a form recalls *disegno* '…in Vasari's sense: the lines which express the mental conception' (Gordon, 1975: 95). This is also reminiscent of Alberti's thoughts on *lineamenta* (1988). The 'Idea' or design is ultimately important in the artistic process, since sketches facilitate concepts. 'Design, then, could mean the expression of the Idea, or conception, or invention; and it could even mean the Idea, or conception, or invention, itself; and could even be regarded, as Zuccari regarded it, as the sign, the stamp of God in man' (Gordon, 1975: 95–97).

The design, *invenzione,* and imagination are simultaneous notions and primary sources of human creativity. This approach was accepted from the time of Plato, through the Renaissance, and again by the Romantics. Alternately, German and British poets and philosophers disagreed and felt 'fancy' and 'imagination' could not be considered the same. One quality of imagination produces a synthesis of something new (a creative act), but not all acts of the imagination are creative. Often the imagination provides only a mental impression from memory, which may not involve anything new. On the other hand, creative acts can also happen through seemingly uncreative methods such as reasoning and intellectual gestation (Casey, 1976).

An unintentional creative act may approach the unexplainable and, consequently, be considered inspiration. The *Oxford English Dictionary* defines 'to inspire' as to breathe or blow into or upon. It also means to simulate creative activity in an act; to bring about or produce. 'Inspiration' thus denotes the ability to make something entirely new or to bring to life.

Leonardo da Vinci suggested that one good method of inspiration was to observe stains on rocks. He felt there were multiple images in those stains, which could provide stimulation for various compositions and scenes. Every child has experienced lying in the grass and finding animals in the shapes of clouds. Likewise, Hubert Damisch has devoted a whole book to the theory of clouds (1972). He uses examples from painting to discuss semiotic issues, and one concept that seems relevant when discussing fantasy comes from this study.

Damisch describes a practice in China of blowing powder through cotton to make images of clouds. It is possible to differentiate between sketchers versus blowers of clouds, in that the sketch is the line on the paper but the cloud – powder blown through cotton – has an incredible vagueness. Damisch likens the vagueness of the cloud to infinity and, consequently, the cloud, then, could be anything; it has endless possibilities. '[A] similar thought in connection with another group of chance configurations – clouds: "The mind's own power to shape now boldly wakes, as definite from indefinite it makes"' (Kris & Kurz, 1979: 47). In play, clouds can be anything they are reminiscent of, or anything the mind can suppose; their infinite vagueness allows for pure possibility.

Fantasy and possibilizing can be accompanied by another aspect of creative inspiration. Andre Breton, a representative of the Surrealist Movement, writes about a game that views creativity in a different way. The game was called the *Exquisite Corpse* (Figure 3.14) and was played in a group, where each player in turn drew a sketch or partial image, turned over the edge of the paper and passed it to the next player (Waldberg, 1965). The resulting image was fantastical, comical and absurd in its incongruous combination. The accidental quality was vital to the strange juxtaposition of images. The *Exquisite Corpse* is not unlike the stains on rocks or cloud formations since they all entail a haphazard image. They are projections onto a vague image, which leads into a more specific (named) image. How the image is eventually perceived depends to a certain degree on the formation of projections onto that image and, similarly, it is an interpretation that allows the mind to comprehend the absurdity of the combination.

One last aspect of fantasy which relates to inspiration involves revelation and eureka. Revelation as a divine disclosure is very similar to inspiration. If a totally random thought occurs to the mind, and it is impossible to understand its origins, it might be easy to find divinity in its origin.

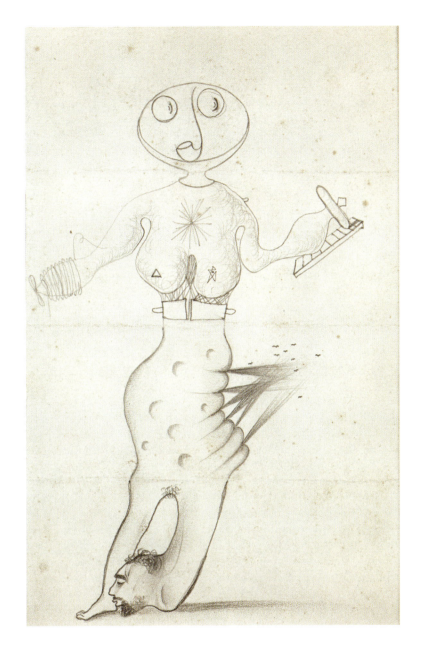

FIGURE 3.14 Y. Tanguy, A. Breton, M. Duhamel, M. Morise; Exquisite Corpse.

Of course, this differs over cultures, periods of history, and personal belief, but the point here is that of unexplained inspiration. The capacity for memory to be retained, and work suddenly with imagination, is exciting and quite unexplained. Thoughts need to overlap for some time in our bodies, as body memory or *mneme*, before an occurrence of 'eureka'. It is conceivable how this activity might work for architects. The associative overlapping can happen visually on paper, sometimes as hands subconsciously scribble. In a similar way, thinking continuously about the project will lead to the solution in the imagination.

This discussion now turns to the wonderful sketches of Sir Norman Foster. An architect with an incredible ability to envision the tall building in context of major cities, his work always

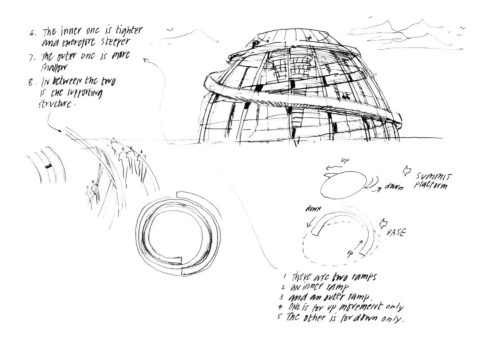

6. The inner one is tighter and therefore steeper
7. The outer one is more shallow
8. In between the two is the supporting structure.

up
down
summit platform
down
BASE
up

1 There are two ramps
2 An inner ramp
3 and an outer ramp.
4 One is for up movement only
5 The other is for down only.

FIGURE 3.15   Sir Norman Foster; Concept sketch.

undertakes the opportunities for a technological approach. His work, once viewed as 'High Tech', is sensitive to innovative structure and materiality. Extremely diverse, his projects include the Hong Kong Shanghai Bank, the Faculty of Law at the University of Cambridge and the New German Parliament (Reichstag) in Berlin. Foster has received many awards from the Royal Institute of British Architects including the Gold Medal. He was awarded the Pritzker Prize in Architecture in 1999 and has received the Premier Architecture Award from the Royal Academy in London, as well as a Knighthood from the Queen of England.

This sketch (Figure 3.15) is a study for the dome of the historic Reichstag. Recognizing humans can imagine 'whatever and however we would like', this sketch explores the form and circulation structure of the dome. Not a sketch concerned with first inspiration, this sketch employs drawing to imagine a difficult form, particularly complex because at the time of the drawing it did not exist. The ramps that flow through the circular space are difficult to visualize. Foster employed words to assist with this difficult task. By diagramming and explaining the flow of pedestrian traffic on the spiral ramps, he was thinking through the three-dimensional problem on a two-dimensional surface. Using spontaneity and controlledness, Foster was pondering the circulation patterns. Depending on the visual for inspiration, he was also limiting his focus. Thinking primarily of the opportunities at hand, he presented the information on one page, not straying from the topic. Opening up the range of possibilities, he has diagrammed the space with simple lines and arrows. Note how the several small sketches encircle the perspective view. The three-dimensional view (even with the context of clouds) tests the 'look' of the final product and the diagrams test the function. In a manner of indeterminacy, the perspective does not completely explain the dome; it remains sufficiently vague to project possible refinement. If a sketch that reveals the future is a fantasy, Foster's sketch articulates a vision of what can be.

A sketch page (Figure 3.16) by Robert Venturi, of the firm Venturi Scott Brown Architects in Philadelphia, Pennsylvania, concludes this chapter with the idea of the imagination as a function of memory as an inspiration for fantasy. This image is a beautifully precise preliminary sketch for the Gordon Wu Hall at Princeton University. On the left side of the page are two façades,

FIGURE 3.16   Robert Venturi; Gordon Wu Hall.

and on the right are variations, possibilities for the design of a detail. Sketched with bold lines from a felt marker, Venturi has articulated historic references onto the façade of the building. The large pediment and exaggerated arches evoke an imaginative use of past to present the future in new form. The clear and definitive lines show Venturi's confidence with the genre and the medium.

The fact that such a precise sketch communicated the historic language in a few lines begins to suggest a caricature. As with a caricature, the sketch finds the most pertinent and salient features to demonstrate intent. The arched features to the right demonstrate a search for form, as if he was using his imagination to explore alternatives to a particular visual identity. The briefness of the sketch shows best in the columns on the elevation – a small circle and a loop. On the column to the right, the loop was left incomplete. It was unnecessary to finish the column as the impression could be evaluated as it is. Also, the quickness necessary to view the entirety for evaluation may have precluded the importance of the finished column. With one stroke the street and adjacent storefronts were placed. The beauty of this sketch is Venturi's ability to refine historic detail to its essence. As imagination can also be defined as an act of recombination, this building incorporates layers of memory, placing elements in new juxtaposition.

Fantasy has a long history in relation to art and inspiration, starting with the argument of rhetoric and its close associate, *invenzione*. The inspiration of the creative person, being so difficult to understand, took on divine proportions. The innate talent for making fantastical images seems to be intuitive and displays skills which add to creative abilities. Although architects use their imaginations to fantasize about that which is unknown, fantasy seems to be something more. The action of sketching seems to facilitate the powers of fantasy to help view new combinations and bring mental impressions forward from memory. The following expresses the exquisite relationship between sketches and fantasy:

> *These drawings should be seen not as the expression of an idea existing in the artist's mind, but rather as a set of initial marks and touches of the crayon, which might freely be developed as ornament, or figures, or articulating members, so that in progressive superimposed drafts, the* concetto *was worked toward a final resolution of elements, according to the artist's* fantasia. *(Summers, 1981: 125)*

Memory, imagination and fantasy drive the activity of sketching. These complex mental faculties are the mind's image-making functions. When sketching, the architect is constructing images whose use depends on anticipation and intentionality. The making of these images stems from memories of past experiences. Reorganized, the images translate experiences into a new form. The sketch becomes the dialogue and also the facilitator of these processes which, because of human touch, is an extension of the thinking faculty for architects.

BIBLIOGRAPHY

Akahira, K. (1982). *Drawings by Japanese Contemporary Architects*. Graphic-sha.

Alberti, L.B. (1988). *On the Art of Building in Ten Books* (translated by J. Rykwert). MIT Press.

Arendt, H. (1971). *Thinking. (Volume I of The Life of the Mind)*. Harcourt Brace Jovanovich.

Aristotle, (1928). *The Works of Aristotle Translated into English* (edited by W.D. Ross). Oxford University Press.

Aristotle, (1935). *De Anima and De Memoria* (translated by W.S. Holt). Harvard University Press.

Aristotle, (1951). *Aristotle's Theory of Poetry and Fine Art*. Dover.

Bachelard, G. (1987). *On Poetic Imagination and Reverie*. Spring Publications.

Barasch, M. (1985). *Theories of Art, From Plato to Winckelmann*. New York University Press.

Beardsley, M.C. (1966). *Aesthetics from Classical Greece to the Present, A Short History*. University of Alabama Press.

Bjork, E.L. and Bjork, R. (1996). *Memory*. Academic Press.

Blackmore, S. (1999). *The Meme Machine*. Oxford University Press.

Bloch, D. (2007). *Aristotle on Memory and Recollection; Text, Translation, Interpretation, and Reception in Western Scholasticism*. Brill.

Brann, T.H. (1991). *The World of Imagination; Sum and Substance*. Rowman and Littlefield.

Bundy, M.W. (1927). *Theory of Imagination in Classical and Medieval Thought*. University of Illinois.

Burnett, R. (2004). *How Images Think*. MIT Press.

Casey, E.S. (1976). *Imagining: A Phenomenological Study*. Indiana University Press.

Casey, E.S. (1987). *Remembering: A Phenomenological Study*. Indiana University Press.

Cicero, (1942). *De Oratore* (translated by E. W. Sutton). The Loeb Classical Library/Heinemann.

Cicero, (1954). *Ad G. Herennium de Ratione Dicendi* (translated by H. Caplan). The Loeb Classical Library/Heinemann.

Collins, A.F. (1993). *Theories of Memory*. L. Erlbaum Assoc.

Damisch, H. (1972). *Theorie Du/Nuagel, Pour une Histoire de la Peinture*. Editions Du Seuil.

Evans, R. (1986). Translations From Drawing to Building. *AA Files*, **12**, pp. 3–18.

Gordon, D.J. (1975). *The Renaissance Imagination*. University of California Press.

Gregory, R.L. (1987). *The Oxford Companion to the Mind*. Oxford University Press.

Hawkins, J. and Blakeslee, S. (2004). *On Intelligence*. Times Books.

Hinton, G. (1979). Some Demonstrations of the Effects of Structural Descriptions in Mental Imagery. *Cognitive Science*, 3, pp. 231–250.

Hume, D. (1978). *A Treatise of Human Nature* (edited by Selby-Bigge, L.A.). Clarendon.

Jung, C.G. (1953 and 1979). *The Collected Works of C.G. Jung, 20 volumes Bollington Series XX* (translated by R.F.C Hull, edited by H. Read, M. Fordham, G. Adler and W. McGuire). Princeton University Press.

Jung, C.G. (1968). *Man and his Symbols*. Dell.

Jung, C.G. (1983). *The Essential Jung: Selected Writings Introduced by Anthony Storr* (selected and introduced by Storr, A.). Princeton University Press.

Kant, I. (1961). *Immanuel Kant's Critique of Pure Reason* (translated by N. Kemp). MacMillan.

Kosslyn, S.M. (1994). *Image and Brain: the resolution of the imagery debate*. MIT Press.

Kris, E. and Kurz, O. (1979). *Legend, Myth and Magic in the Image the Artist*. Yale University Press.

Le Corbusier (1981). *Le Corbusier Sketchbooks Volumes*, 1–4. MIT Press.

Merleau-Ponty, M. (1962). *Phenomenology of Perception* (translated by C. Smith). The Humanities Press.

Plato, (1941). *Republic* (translated by B. Jowett). Walter J. Black.

Plato, (1953). *The Dialogues of Plato* (translated by B. Jowett). Oxford University Press.

Ricoeur, P. (2004). *Memory, History, Forgetting*. University of Chicago Press.

Schacter, D.L. (1996). *Searching for Memory: the Brain, the Mind, and the Past*. Basic Books.

Schaefer, D.L. (2001). *The Seven Sins of Memory: how the mind forgets and remembers*. Houghton Mifflin.

Summers, D. (1981). *Michelangelo and the Language of Art*. Princeton University Press.

Tulving, E. and Craik, F. (2000). *The Oxford Handbook of Memory*. Oxford University Press.

Vasari, G. (1946). *Lives of the Artists* (abridged and edited by Burroughs, B.). Simon and Schuster.

Verene, D. (1987). Philosophical Memory. *AA Files*, **16**, pp. 57–62.

Waldberg, P. (1965). *Surrealism*. Oxford University Press.

Ward, T.B., Smith, S.M. and Vaid, J. (1997). *Creative Thought: An Investigation of Conceptual Structures and Processes*. American Psychology Association.

Warnock, M. (1976). *Imagination*. University of California Press.

White, A.R. (1990). *The Language of Imagination*. Basil Blackwell.

Wittkower, R. and Wittkower, M. (1963). *Born Under Saturn; The Character and Conduct of Artists: A Documented History From Antiquity to the French Revolution*. W.W. Norton.

Yates, F. (1966). *The Art of Memory*. University of Chicago Press.

Zevi, B. (1999). *Erich Mendelsohn; The Complete Works*. Birkhauser.

CHAPTER 4

CARICATURE AS A MODE OF TRANSFORMATION

By virtue of its wit and intelligence, this sketch by Eric Kahn (Figure 4.1) may resemble a caricature. It is poignant in its method of communication as it locates the unique essence of form relationships. In this sketch Kahn employs lines that are exuberant. The swirled marks are so tremendously abstract that they could be mountains, waterfalls, foliage, or dancing figures.

The loose lines dance across the page seemingly denying boundaries. Although it may appear Kahn was doodling or scribbling, the intention of the sketch can be seen in the repeated forms and areas of concentration. The sketch may have been a method to quickly visualize form, proportion and volume before committing to a particular composition. The abstraction may have allowed Kahn to see the basic volumes and find associative shapes in these sketches that have been completed with great energy. This may suggest that he sketched arbitrarily in order to preclude any connection with intention. The repeating shapes indicate a theme or search for a way to represent a vague form in his mind's eye.

Kahn writes about the sketches: 'Gothic tracery, lines of force and specific materiality *drifts*. Sets of lines gain new materiality and behavior; bundled tight, unbundled and loosened, control confronts disarray, the dense weave is undone and redone.' Profoundly metaphorical, the images reference an ephemeral interpretation. As allusions, these sketches appeal to emotions and thus reveal a more complex meaning not initially apparent. They capture an essence that may be hard to define. Although the intention of the sketches was not necessarily caricature, their search for interpretation may find a truth in the purpose.

Some qualities of architectural sketches can be understood more easily when perceived as caricatures. Sketches are quick and, in their quickness, can display combinations of elements which would be impossible in other types of drawings. Architects employ these brief drawings to spark their imagination, to communicate, to think through a detail or to convince a client. As convincing and quickly apprehended visual devices, sketches that are conceived as caricatures provide the viewer with a richer context than might be expected. These include sketches: as sub-themes, as architectural details acting to caricature a building, containing borrowed sources, caricaturing another building either by the architect or by another architect, as manifestations of self-reflexivity, as caricature of the finished work, or as metaphorical references. Often the sketches may be comprehended as elements of ridicule and satire, where they become modes of critical humor. Understanding the architectural sketch as caricature opens the reading of sketches to interpretations that may otherwise be overlooked.[1]

---

[1] Aspects of this chapter were explored in the article: Smith, K.S. (1990). Architectural Sketches and the Power of Caricature. *Journal of Architectural Education*, 44:1, pp. 49–58.

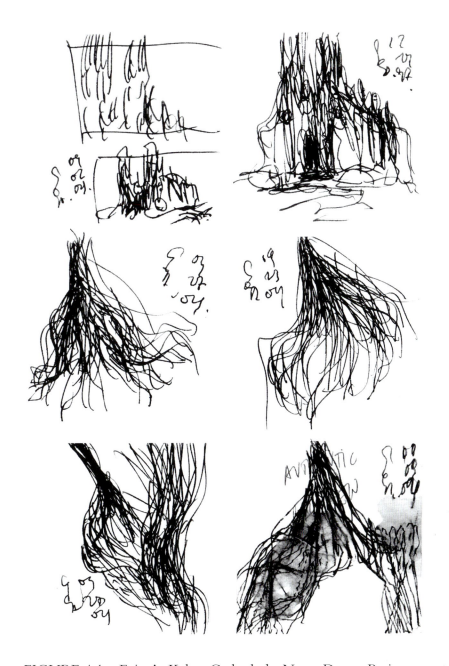

FIGURE 4.1   Eric A. Kahn; Cathedrals: Notre Dame, Paris 2004.

HISTORY OF CARICATURE

Historically, caricature is difficult to distinguish from illustration or comical art. In his book *A History of Caricature and Grotesque in Literature and Art*, Thomas Wright gives evidence of caricature in Egypt. He writes of an example in which a scene shows a small boat with provisions that runs into the back of a larger funeral boat, upsetting the tables of cakes and other supplies (1968).

Other Egyptian examples show animals employed in occupations usually reserved for humans. This role reversal, demonstrating the impossible notion of animals assuming human tasks, is humorous (Wright, 1968).

Wright discusses examples of Greek and Roman satiric drama in which parody shows in masks, and a sculpture in which a Gaul is presented '...thrusting out his tongue in a very unbecoming manner' (1968). He writes of how the Greeks parodied sacred subjects; even their gods were treated with disrespect in pictorial representation. In another example, Pompeiian drawings picture pygmies or dwarfs with extremely large heads and very small arms and legs (Wright, 1968).

The Middle Ages provide examples of carnivals, festivals and enjoyment of the ludicrous. A manuscript from this time provides an example of two demons tripping a monk and throwing him in a river. This burlesque is evident in the Middle Ages' idea of the world turned upside down. Another example is a drawing of a blacksmith where a goose has taken the place of a horse and he is nailing a shoe on the webbed foot (Wright, 1968). These examples from the Middle Ages seem to interchange humorous art with that of caricature.

Other more recent researchers suggest that caricature is a relatively recent art. Ernst Gombrich and Ernst Kris have undertaken a comprehensive study of caricature. In their research, they discover a rebirth of caricature, as opposed to humorous art, in that portrait caricature was uncommon before the end of the sixteenth century. For them the '...conscious distortion of the features of a person with the aim of ridicule' is substantially different from comic art (Kris & Gombrich, 1938). Although satirical writing was prevalent prior to the Renaissance, the Gombrich and Kris study questioned why artists had not used caricature:

The belief in the magical sign and the thing signified is deepest rooted in pictorial art. Whilst words are easier understood as conventional signs which one can play with, alter and change without affecting the essence of the being they signify, a picture remains for us for all time a sort of double, which we dare not damage for fear that we might injure the person or being itself. Image-magic is perhaps the most widespread of all spells. (Kris & Gombrich, 1938: 339)

Particularly in Renaissance Italy, artists were revered as creators and given credit for talent rather than being a tool of the church. An explanation lies partly in a shift of their role in society. This esteemed position meant that they were valuable, and powerful people sought their talent and expertise. The artist possessed '...the supreme right of the poet, to form a reality of his own' (Kris & Gombrich, 1938: 331). The work of art was viewed as a projection of an inner image, and these fanciful ideas and combinations emerged from the imagination of the artists themselves. Gombrich and Kris acknowledge the new respect for the artist's individual talent: '[i]magination rather than technical ability, vision and invention, inspiration and genius made the artist, not merely the mastering of the intricacies of handicraft' (Kris & Gombrich, 1938: 331).

The nature of caricature depends upon memory, imagination and fantasy. The use of ridicule originates from a memory of specific characteristics of a figure. Likewise, memory assists viewer's to recognize and understand humor, because they also know from memory the figure's peculiarities. The imagination of caricaturists demonstrates the techniques of transformation, ambiguity and condensation, which they employ to ridicule and expose the true personality of their subjects (Kris & Gombrich, 1938).

Imagination may be engaged as the caricaturist must formulate and recombine visual forms to expose an underlying truth. In a similar way, fantasy reinforces the strange juxtaposition of the two-dimensional drawn visual forms, which may be referred to as 'images', and the disintegration of deformation. To elucidate this deformation in the ridicule of caricature, Gombrich and Kris, in another collaboration about caricature, discuss an artist whom they perceive as the first or foremost caricaturist – Annibale Carracci (1560–1609):

It was in the first place a discovery concerning the nature of likeness. To put it briefly, it was the discovery that similarity is not essential to likeness. The deliberate distortion of single features is not incompatible with a striking likeness in the whole. True caricature in this new sense is not content with drawing a long nose just a little longer, or a broad chin just a bit broader. Such partial distortions are characteristic only of superficial or immature work. The real aim of the true caricaturist is to transform the whole man into a completely new and ridiculous figure which nevertheless resembles the original in a striking and surprising way. (Gombrich & Kris, 1940: 12)

Annibale and Agostino Carracci are credited with naming these altered portraits *ritrattina carichi*, meaning 'loaded portraits'. The historic popularity of caricature is revealed by a 1646 *Trattato* in which A. Mosini provided a definition of caricature. Other Renaissance artists practicing this art included Pier Leone Ghezzi, Giovanni Bracelli and Gian Lorenzo Bernini. Furthermore, Bernini was the sculptor and architect who had been attributed with transporting the concept of caricature to France in the seventeenth century (Horn, 1980).

It was Thomas Brown who introduced the term *caricature* to England, and other famous caricaturists include Thomas Rowlandson, James Gillray and William Hogarth's (1697–1764) elaborate caricature series starting with 'A Harlot's Progress' in 1732. Honoré Daumier and Charles Philipon drew political cartoons in France; especially notable is 'the pear king Louis-Philippe'. Americans also produced early political cartoons, notably those of Benjamin Franklin (Horn, 1980). Other parts of the world, such as Japan, also embraced comic and caricature art, but many of these images take the form of humor rather than caricature.

More recently, Charles Baudelaire explored the philosophical notion of the comic and caricature. He wrote about the nature of their methods, irony and sarcasm, understatement and extravagance, violence and insinuation, and farce and wit (Hannoosh 1992). He expressed the low and coarse in contrast to the extraordinary aesthetic importance of art. This dualism accents that laughter contains a measure of pain, reminding humans of their '…inferiority and mortality, of the dualism necessary to art, and thus of our potential for transcendence' (Hannoosh, 1992). Architects, similar to artists, understand the multiple levels on which sketches convey impressions.

DEFINITION OF CARICATURE

A caricature expressed by transformation and deformation emphasizes a certain characteristic of a person, animal, or thing which captures or helps us understand a specific personality. The role of caricature in revealing a truth has occasional affinity to a monster (Frascari, 1991). A caricature stresses specific aspects of a concept, and more of the image is involved, but both caricature and monsters recombine complex narratives or forms into new compositions; these compositions convey a new meaning. Where caricature demonstrates and employs the new combination 'to show', the monster presents the future and acts as a soothsayer in the role of architecture. A caricature, on the contrary, emphasizes deformation to disclose the true state of affairs, to ascertain the inner nature of a specific personality, or, most often, to ridicule.

Caricature takes important aspects of the character to the extreme so that the character's visual likeness is recognized. To reiterate, caricature depends on the combination of unique characteristics and the transformation of features. The transformation of dynamic features of the likeness must rely on the ability of that counterpart to emerge from behind to be recognized. Part of the humor and understanding is conveyed through the caricature's resemblance to the corresponding shape: '[r]esemblance is a prerequisite of caricature' (Kris, 1934: 298).

The interpretation, or understanding of a caricature surprises the viewer by its recognition, simplicity, and its quickness. This recognition, often in the form of humor, permeates architectural sketches. They are quick in reference to play, meaning intelligent and also witty. Caricature has a strong relationship to play and, similar to qualities of quickness, the conceptual nature of architecture is revealed by architects who possess the skills of narrative, speed of mind, ability to express their

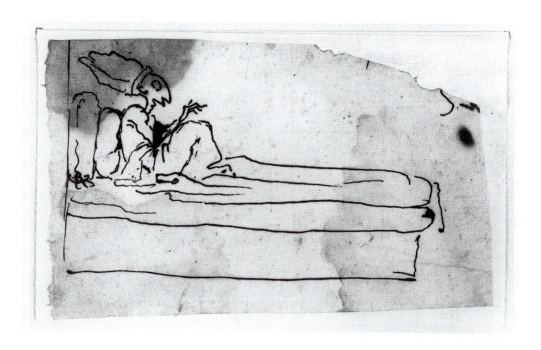

FIGURE 4.2   Gianlorenzo Bernini; A caricature of a Cardinal in bed.

thoughts, possess a sense of time, and understand the essence of economy (Calvino, 1988). Architects' experience, humor, and imagination help them to achieve caricature in their work.

A sketch by Gianlorenzo Bernini (Figure 4.2) reveals some of these skills of the caricaturist. Although not an architectural subject, this sketch is particularly interesting in that Bernini was an artist, sculptor and architect. It questions Bernini's attitude toward the power of drawing to elicit an underlying determination whether the subject is architectural or artistic. Here Bernini sketches the character of Cardinal Borghese and even though this drawing dates from the late Renaissance or early Baroque period, it is possible to detect the cleverness and humor used to describe the Cardinal's face. Often a caricature requires knowledge of the original, but in this sketch Bernini captures the personality in such a way that it is possible to identify the ridicule in this telling portrait.

In a less than dignified position, Cardinal Borghese has been pictured on a sedan or in bed. He wears an extraordinarily large *mitre*; although it defines his position, its size has been exaggerated as it nearly slides off the back of his head. Cardinals were occasionally allowed to wear this headgear but the *mitre* was usually designated for the Pope and bishops, as part of formal regalia. Wearing the *mitre* to bed or in a casual way may have been a sarcastic commentary on the attitudes of Cardinal Borghese. Bernini's slow pen lines express a confidence in the form composed in his mind. With a single line he was able to outline the Cardinal's entire head and neck, with an extremely large nose and thin neck. The line-thin fingers are posed in a declarative gesture, possibly another point of ridicule. Bernini has drawn the eye of Borghese in profile with a single circle. Remarkably, the pupil of the eye has been implied by the slight thickness of line where the circle terminates. Hunched, and nearly reclining, the narrative expresses a feeble and ineffective cleric. Here the caricature provides the expression of an understanding with only a few lines. Kris and Gombrich comment on these revealing features when they write about other of Bernini's caricature drawings:

The strokes of his pen show a sublime freedom. Following the lines of the compositions we realize that it was not by chance that this style came to be used for caricature, for it belongs to the essence of the joke and can scarcely be separated from its inner meaning. The physiognomical expression in the fine drawing of a captain of the fire brigade becomes a grin, and this grin consists of a single line. The face of Cardinal Scipione Borghese is distilled down to a few lines as if it were restricted to a formula. Thus, the abbreviated style gains its own significance, as if the artist were to say to us: 'See, this great man is nothing but a lot of lines; I can grasp his personality in a few strokes'. (Kris & Gombrich, 1938: 324)

Conveying a concept quickly, especially one that expresses a truth in ridicule, is distinctive of caricature, as it reflects a skill of economy, expressing the most with the least. Caricature assists, through visual recognition, in the immediate interpretation of a person or situation that is often elusive and lies beneath the surface, available to be released by humor and ridicule. Gombrich and Kris discuss caricature's hidden meaning in evaluating the artist Carracci:

Is not the caricaturist's task, he is reported to have said, exactly the same as the classical artist's? Both see the lasting truth beneath the surface of mere outward appearance…The one may strive to visualize the perfect form and to realize it in his work, the other to grasp the perfect deformity, and thus reveal the very essence of a personality. (Gombrich & Kris, 1940: 11, 12)

Ridicule is the characteristic of caricature that separates it from parody or humorous art (Hutcheon, 1985). Although characteristics of these genres are often interchangeable, along with those of the grotesque, a definition of ridicule can provide an understanding of its intricacies. To ridicule is commonly defined as to mock, to show the absurdity of, to make fun of, belittle, taunt or tease. Looking more closely, its meaning also includes to gouge and to expose (Oxford English Dictionary). These meanings assist in understanding the importance of ridicule in caricature. Ridicule in caricature makes use of critical humor to find the faults in a character in order to exaggerate them. This exposure of otherwise subtle characteristics finds a truth beneath an illusory façade. To gouge may mean to poke holes in; another way to find a truth and see underneath. The etymology of ridicule is very close to that of riddle. *Raedels* means opinion or conjecture, and *raedan* is to advise, interpret, guess, penetrate or pierce (Oxford English Dictionary). All of these terms point to the revelatory aspects of caricature. To riddle can mean to make holes in, or to separate. In this instance, the riddle associated with ridicule sifts out a new interpretation or critical comment.

As mentioned earlier, Annibale and Agostino Carracci named these critical exaggerations *ritrattina carichi*. A look at the Italian meaning of *caricatura* finds a relationship to load, burden or exaggerate. The ridicule of caricature may 'load' the image with multiple interpretations. This extra information contained in a caricature may express more knowledge than an illusionary portrait. Caricature's meaning 'to burden' also provides a relationship to satire, which is directly related to ridicule. *Satura* means 'full' and is related to *satis* which means 'enough'. Satire is often considered interchangeable with ridicule and the aspects of 'full' and 'loaded' from caricature give the ridicule a dimension of containing immense meaning (Oxford English Dictionary). Gombrich and Kris further describe the hidden meaning found in the deformation of caricature when they write that the features of the caricature seem like a mask, but the exaggeration serves to unmask the victim (1938). Caricature removes a façade, and allows a view beneath it; in this sense it resembles the grotesque by revealing a new truth in the reality it displays.

The grotesque is an intermediary between the known and the unknown, as it straddles two worlds. Its transient ambivalence is incoherent and concedes multiple interpretations (Harpham, 1982). Geoffrey Harpham explains that 'grotesqueries' are literary or visual occurrences which '…[call] into question the adequacy of our ways of organizing the world, of dividing the continuum of experience into knowable particles' (1982: 3). The grotesque resembles caricature in that both approaches to representation exhibit intelligence, often through paradox (Harpham, 1982). The immediate recognition is contingent upon interpretation.

With art, and comparably to architectural sketches, this immediacy tends to make the physical image expendable. The abstract thoughts generated, the forms conceived and allusions discovered constitute the importance of sketching but, after the thought process is complete, sketches are only leftover physical fragments of the design. The procedure of caricature is similar, in that once a caricature's meaning is recognized, the message is known and it may not be necessary to use the caricature again. The narrative of a caricature recounts the story of the person because, in its economy of lines, the caricature gives insight into the deeds or position of a figure. It also requires intelligence and wit to find truth in a fleeting expression.

The caricaturist finally, and probably most importantly, needs imagination to transform and combine, so it is possible to understand this new interpretation. With this communication to someone, the caricaturist must have some dimension of intention. That intention may be strong, as expressed in a political cartoon, or as subtle as Michelangelo's placing an eye on his drawing of a molding profile (Figure 3.8). Ridicule is intentional by nature because of the necessity to include some aspect of the original in the caricature. Because the caricature is visual, its intentions must be inferred from the image (the text). Since there is no record of intention other than the caricature, its effectiveness depends on the perceiver. It is necessary to borrow from the original to communicate the meaning of the ridicule. Since caricature is not a replica, or quotation, the relationship to the original requires interpretation.

CARICATURE EVIDENT IN ARCHITECTURAL SKETCHES

Architects deforming images may not recognize the communication of a caricature as ridicule. The visual comment could be seen as simply a translation of the original. This type of intention is dominant in architecture, where buildings contain elements of precedent, such as Robert Venturi's sketch of the Gordon Wu Hall (Figure 3.16). Contrarily, the knowledge of the perceiver determines the meaning, which may or may not be understood. The difference between caricature and an imitation of precedent is ridicule, whether intentional or unintentional. The intention to demonstrate something more than an illusionary image comprises the loading and exposing of ridicule (Hutcheon, 1985).

Having introduced concepts of caricature, it is necessary to consider what it discloses about architectural sketches. Many questions arise about deformation's relationship to the image, and how and why the ridicule and deformation of buildings by architects when sketching help the architect better understand architecture and apply imagination. It is possible because sketches are a pliable medium; quick, graphically incomplete and vague, they do not destroy the building in transformation. The play qualities of sketches may allow for uninhibited ridicule, which may or may not transfer to the completed building. Seldom do architects sketch their buildings in their entirety; often the whole cannot be enlarged to see the specificity of the parts. Even when studying details, architects comprehend the whole, and a single element can reveal the concepts of the entire building.

A second sketch by the Italian architect Carlo Scarpa demonstrates how a detail can be reflected in the whole (Figure 4.3). This page is scattered with plans, details, diagrams and three-dimensional studies for the restaurant at the Castelvecchio Museum in Verona. Each image appears to contain a similar theme but has been studied at different scales. The largest drawing, placed in the center and possibly rendered first, is a plan articulating wall relationships. In various parts of the drawing can be seen the reveals that form interstitial spaces. An architectural 'reveal' (the void between two elements) has been traditionally used to separate two diverse construction materials. In the plan this concept is echoed where Scarpa pulls the walls away from each other in an effort to accent the space between. These relationships seem to notch into each other creating interconnected spaces that have been studied below the plan and in three-dimensions to the lower left of the sheet.

On another scale, the top and right sides (both top and bottom) of the page display construction details of a similar theme. These connectors are bent, curved, and bind negative spaces of similar shape. The distances between the materials create a certain tension in the internal volume.

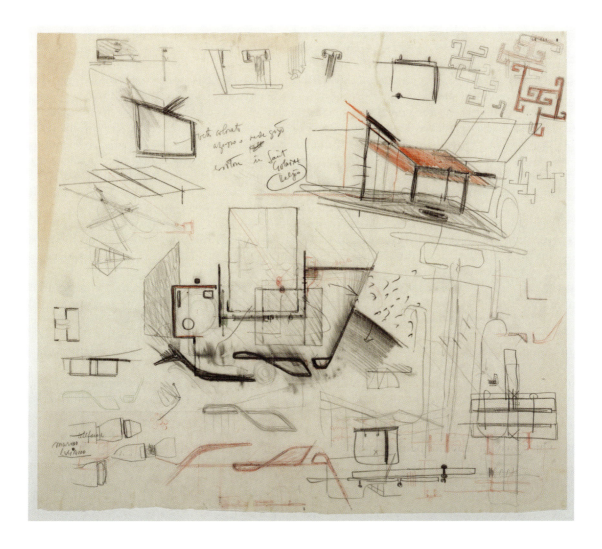

FIGURE 4.3   Carlo Scarpa; Schizzi vari per un allestimento.

The detail reinforces what the building is, and brings out its meaning through caricature. This is not so surprising since the concepts of the whole, the thoughts in Scarpa's mind, are unified and revealed throughout. Kris and Gombrich write about an important feature of caricature: '[h]ere, too, a single feature often stands for the whole, and a person is represented by one salient characteristic only' (1938: 325). Features characteristically reminiscent can be treated similarly in a sketch because their likeness in treatment becomes a caricature.

A sketch, which demonstrates what architects think, can also caricature natural elements as metaphors. Architects draw images they are familiar with and alter or deform them either to create new forms or to understand those they are drawing. Kris and Gombrich further define the role of caricature for the artist:

…whereas the artist, although the most alive of all men to external stimuli, is nevertheless a person who elaborates, plays with and reshapes sensory experience under the influence of internal and affective states. With the turn of the century came a new means of grasping the ways in which the mind plays with elements of sensory experience and out of them shapes new patterns. (Kris & Gombrich, 1938: 319)

Metaphors can also provide a conceptual beginning for architecture, and are closely related to caricature, since caricature references an original in some form. This sketch by Jørn Utzon (Figure 4.4) explores a cloud metaphor to envision a ceiling for the Bagsvaerd Church in Bagsvaerd, Denmark. The Danish architect Jørn Utzon is known for his graceful and poetic sculptural forms that are responsive to individual conditions of site. Currently joined by his sons in the firm Utzon Associates Architects, he has completed a wide variety of projects from housing to monumental civic buildings. In 1957 he won the competition for a new Opera House in Sydney, Australia. Since that time he has completed such projects as the Planetstaden housing project in Lund, Sweden; the National Assembly of Kuwait; Bagsvaerd Community Church, in 1976; and the celebrated design of his house, Can Feliz in Majorca, Spain. Utzon has been awarded many honors such as the 2003 Pritzker Prize in Architecture, the C.F. Hansen Medal for Architecture, and Gold Medals from the Royal Australian Institute of Architects and the Royal Institute of British Architects.

This page represents two sketches by Utzon for the Bagsvaerd Community Church. In a very clear reference, he has, on the left, sketched a beach scene with billowy clouds and, on the right, an interior space. Utzon rendered these perspectives in a soft medium, such as chalk or crayon, using a brilliant blue for the sky and water. In both sketches he sets figures in the middle of the space, bounded from above by clouds and by earth below. The comparison is certainly meant to be analogous. But the reference may also be metaphoric, where the ceiling is a cloud. It is possible that Utzon used this pair of sketches to explain a concept to the parishioners, but it may also have been to convince himself of the scene he was envisioning. He may have needed to visualize the perspective and the closeness of the clouds to create an interior space. As light speaks of a heavenly body in ecclesiastical architecture, these clouds may help worshipers raise their attentions to the sky.

A sketch presents a quick method to confirm the metaphor, with enough ambiguity to render the comparison plausible. The techniques of the sketches are sufficiently alike as to reinforce the

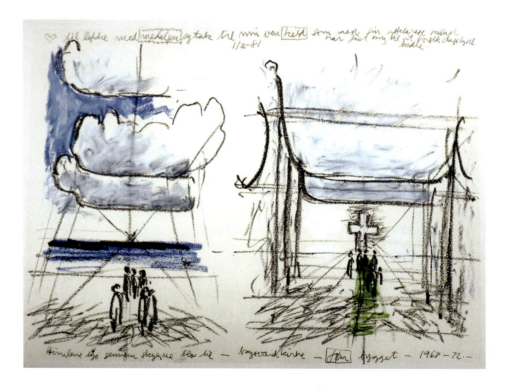

FIGURE 4.4   Jørn Utzon; Bagsvaerd Community Church.

relationship. As the scene on the left focuses attention on the horizon, the interior space focuses on the transparent cross. The sketch on the right, although not necessarily evoking ridicule, certainly simplifies and deforms the scene to comprehend the comparison and thus the intelligence.

When architects employ sketches to explore abstract concepts, their sketches contain individual value. To discover a beginning point or work through a detail, some architects first draw images they are familiar with to start cognitive analogies. Because these first drawings are loose and simple, the architect does not need to be concerned with the delicacies of connection. As in a caricature, the austere, vague forms allow the artist to combine, for example, a human's body and a goat's head. The metamorphosis – the transformation of human into animal, or animal into human – is common in caricature. With similar change, '[t]he Carracci transformed the portraits of their friends into pots, lanterns or barrels' (Kris & Gombrich, 1938: 334). This transformation can change a human into an animal but still retains the likeness. The following example illustrates this caricature of physiognomy.

This famous group of human profiles by Leonardo da Vinci demonstrates some explorations of physiognomy (Figure 4.5). Leonardo was a fervent observer of his environment. He used observation as a method to understand the nature of the world around him. This empirical approach was the basis for much of his artwork and the 'research' in his notebooks. Being a painter, sculptor, city planner, fortress designer, inventor, and architect, Leonardo understood the importance of *likeness* in all these disciplines, and thus approached each with a similar purpose.

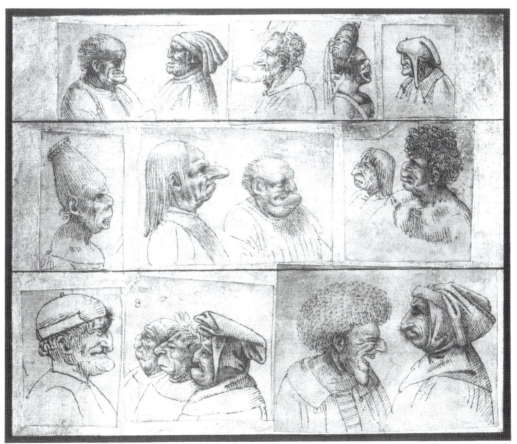

12806 MILANO - Studio - Leonardo da Vinci? - Pinac. Ambrosiana - *Anderson. Roma*

FIGURE 4.5   Leonardo da Vinci; Study of Heads (pen and ink on paper).

These human head profiles may have been drawn entirely from observation. If that was the case, he located an unusually large assemblage of deformed specimens for study. Unlike many of his contemporaries, ideal beauty was less important than rendering the uniqueness that he observed. This was partially because much of the purpose of his work benefited his own understanding rather than presentation. Since physiognomy can be defined as a comparison of appearances to character, this group of head studies by Leonardo may have been an inquiry into human nature in relation to character (Swain and Boyes-Stones, 2007). These heads have been placed on one sheet, not pasted together as a collection. This would imply a focus and theme to their compilation. His fascination with the deformed or exaggerated may have emerged from applying this rigorous methodology. Inspecting these profiles, it is possible to recognize comparison to various animals. The beak-like or pug noses, the absent or elongated chins allude to non-human traits. It is possible that he chose these heads because of the caricature he viewed in their actual forms, or he deformed or exaggerated their features to capture the reference to other mammals. It is also plausible that he found interest in the transformation of their features into the extreme as caricature, thus conveying the depth of their personalities.

In another reference to physiognomy, this sketch by the Spanish architect, artist and engineer Santiago Calatrava (Figure 4.6) finds the reference of human form to understand the character of dynamic and metaphorical allusion for structural elements. Calatrava, with a background in Fine Art, received his Ph.D. in Civil Engineering in 1979. He established his reputation with bridge projects such as the Alamillo Bridge and Viaduct and the Campo Volantin Footbridge in Bilbao.

FIGURE 4.6   Santiago Calatrava; Human/Structure sketches.

The office of Santiago Calatrava L.L.C. has completed projects such as the BCE Place Hall in Toronto; the Oriente Railway Station in Lisbon; the Sondica Airport in Bilbao; the expansion of the Milwaukee Art Museum; and the Athens Olympic Sports Complex. He has been awarded numerous honors including the Gold Medal of the Institute of Structural Engineers; the Gold Medal for Merit in the Fine Arts, Ministry of Culture, Spain; membership in the *Les Artes et Lettres*, Paris; and the AIA Gold Medal.

In this sketch a chain of human forms can be seen across the top of the page. The other image on the page is a single male form with defined muscular structure. The figures have been sketched in graphite with watercolor to render volume. On top of the row of figures are u-shaped pieces that refer to webs in a structural system. Here, Calatrava was not necessarily distorting or mimicking a structural form, but instead equating the character and inherent nature of human bodies in tension. If compared to caricature, the bodies are not deformed, rather the positioning and abstraction suggests a relationship between the two – body and structural system – revealing a disposition of the figures. This intrinsic truth has been displayed visually to make its meaning more vivid. Seeing the muscles and understanding the nature of human anatomy assists Calatrava to envision this relationship. Although knowledgeable of the concepts, the visual indicators 'prove' to him the appropriate proportions. Interestingly, in the sketch of the large central figure, the presence of the human head has been diminished by drawing it bent forward. This technique of abstraction strengthens the comparison to a structural system and simplifies the figure to its essence, a method distinctive of caricature. The intentional distortion displays the intelligence of the architect through the metaphoric allusion.

Returning to the page of sketches by Jun Itami (Figure 2.5), it is possible to recognize an architect's reference to history or to work by another architect. Itami recalls the form, heavy concrete walls, domed space, and the eye/hand symbol so distinctive of architect Le Corbusier. This reference to Le Corbusier could not be accidental. The reuse may not represent ridicule, but the transformation certainly suggests a pursuit of distinguishing character. This example may exhibit how architects caricature other buildings, whether as precedent, analysis or imitation. Kris and Gombrich support this notion when they explain how an artist caricatures a figure. 'He [the artist] consciously alters his model, distorts it, plays with its features, and thus shows the power of his imagination – which can exalt as well as degrade' (Kris & Gombrich, 1938: 338).

Using imagination to locate the essence of the figure with a minimal number of lines has traditionally been distinctive of caricature. In Figure 4.7 swift lines create an entire impression without the accuracy of details. This sketch, by Rafael Viñoly for the Van Andel Institute, shows the energetic lines of an architect wanting to see a quick volume to explore relative shapes. Born in Uruguay, Viñoly first began his practice in Argentina. In 1983, he founded Rafael Viñoly Architects PC in New York City. Defying a specific style, his sensitive work responds distinctly to

FIGURE 4.7 Rafael Viñoly; Van Andel Institute project sketch.

individual site conditions and programs. The types of buildings in his portfolio are equally diverse with such projects as the Tokyo International Forum; the Kimmel Center for the Performing Arts in Philadelphia; the Cleveland Museum of Art; the Howard Hughes Medical Institute; the National Institutes of Health at the University of California; and the Samsung Jong-Ro Tower in Seoul. Viñoly is a Fellow in the American Institute of Architects and has been honored for many of his projects. An educator and practitioner his dedication to the development of young architects is evidenced in his office's Research Fellowship program.

The simplicity and unfinished qualities of this drawing do not encourage a questioning of how the connections can actually be accomplished. Although the element of reality is small, the fantasy remains believable. Kris and Gombrich explain this important element of caricature: 'soon, however, a new feature was added which has ever since then constituted one of the essentials of caricature, namely simplification' (1938: 324). A fast line is one that confidently defines a form with smooth uninterrupted flow. Speed can also show in the way the ends of lines return and lift off the page. Also, in identifying a swift line, it is possible to view a continuous stream, since taking the pen off the page requires time. It also may demonstrate fast thinking to synthesize forms and make intelligent connections. Quick lines, also, are less rectangular since changing the direction of the stroke requires a hesitation.

The organizing feature of the page is a pyramid-shaped form edged by scalloped lines. The less distinct building appears as a volume in the center. In an apparent effort to provide context, Viñoly has filled in with looped marks that quickly replicate foliage. The trees and bushes are shown as M's and reversed N's. These beautiful fluid lines undulate in different directions to represent various kinds of background. The diagonal zigzag marks could be bushes, on the lower left and tighter, these lines could represent smaller plants. To the right, the lines turn more horizontal to suggest grass or pavement. These wonderful lines actually appear continuous, as if Viñoly never lifted the pen as he articulated the various foreground and background elements. Here, the simplification gives him a quick image that assists him to visualize the form of the building in context.

In a second sketch from Michael Rotondi, the proportional caricature reflects from section to elevation or in reverse. Obviously, in the convention of architectural drawing, elevations and sections have some commensurable relationships and, although not universally true, floor plates or fenestration patterns correspond from interior to exterior. Looking at Figure 4.8 it is possible to see a series of sketches, elevation, section and three-dimensional views of the Architecture and Art building at Prairie View A&M University in Texas. The page, drawn with pencil, consists of various views accompanied by verbal description – words to further explain orientation or materials.

This sketch speaks of a concern for the whole where façades and internal spaces correlate. His light hand renders thoughtful lines, as if attempting to understand the building through the drawing. Even though a sketch is very seldom a direct relationship between conceptual stages of design and the finished building, here it appears Rotondi was designing the interior volume simultaneously with the exterior. The horizontal stratification, in the top sketch, does not factor so prominently in the completed building. These horizontal lines, of what appears to be an elevation, anticipate the layers of the floors in the section and three-dimensional view. The second sketch is a section indicated by how Rotondi used poché to define the internal volume. In instances where the theme of the building is strong, the different elements are certain to reveal similarities. Although not necessarily intentional, imitating an approach from one sketch to another acts to caricature the whole.

Often a sketch can be a caricature of the drawing itself, or of the drawing that the architect is perceiving as the building, an example of which is a sketch by Denise Scott Brown (Figure 4.9). Denise Scott Brown is a partner with Robert Venturi of Venturi Scott Brown Architects in Philadelphia, and their joint projects have been related earlier. Scott Brown, with expertise in urban design, brings to the partnership a depth of planning experience. This sketch is a study for the façade of the Lewis Thomas Laboratory at Princeton University. It has been drawn in ink on tracing paper with bold single lines. The façade demonstrates symmetrical window patterning, and the windows on the top level are efficient in their basic rendition of fenestration. The street level has been detailed to indicate an arched doorway and large windows.

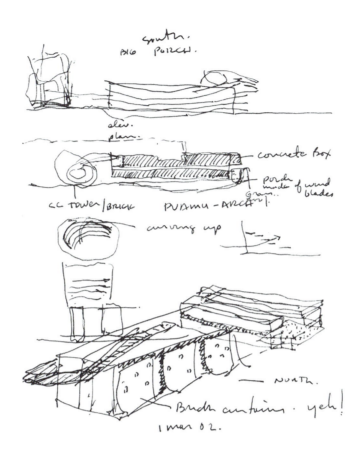

FIGURE 4.8   Michael Rotondi; PVAMU Float. 'Question: is it possible to build a big brick wall that floats in between HEAVY and LIGHT?'

FIGURE 4.9   Denise Scott Brown; Lewis Thomas Laboratory, Princeton University.

The left half of the sketch is more finished than the right half. This would suggest that Scott Brown is right-handed and began on the left side of the page. Beginning to draw on the left side of a sheet is common since it keeps the drawing medium from being smeared. This assumption is particularly pertinent with this sketch because the architectural elements on the left side are more complete than on the right. The checkerboard pattern of tiles has been emphasized with some darker portions; by comparison, the right side has been left as a grid. The same is true with several of the windows, begun to the left and eliminated on the right. This may suggest that once Scott Brown had drawn the basic elements of the design and perceived how they would appear, she only needed to see a caricature of the remaining features to understand, and form judgments about, the whole combination of lines. The sketch may then caricature itself, particularly because what was discovered in one half of a symmetrical building need not be discovered again. One half was sufficient to understand the entire façade.

A sketch from the architectural practice schmidt hammer lassen in Denmark reinforces the proposal that architects caricature their own buildings and those by other architects. This sketch by Morten Schmidt creates a three-dimensional environment through the use of bold horizontal lines (Figure 4.10). The project is the Aarhus Museum of Modern Art in Denmark and the sketch portrays a distinctive feature of the building. The building has been sliced creating a crevice that acts as an atrium. The interior curved ramps, each convex to the atrium, create a tension in the interstitial space. The ramps in the finished building are constructed of smooth concrete, but the multiple parallel lines, in the sketch, present a vibrating energy to the space. A rendered perspective of the completed atrium would in actuality reveal only a few lines, but Schmidt's sketch concentrates on the intended activity of the relationship between the two arced elements. The sketch was completed in a minimal amount of time, as the lines do not hesitate, they are remarkably unwavering, and snap back on themselves. The figures in the space are small verticals intercepting the horizontals, caricaturing

FIGURE 4.10   Morten Schmidt; Aarhus Museum of Modern Art, ARoS.

only one quality of human form. With this image, Schmidt was utilizing simplification and distortion to emphasize the importance of horizontal rows and to caricature the building.

Schmidt's sketch is also reminiscent of images by Erich Mendelsohn of such buildings as Columbushaus and the Government Hospital in Haifa. Like those by Schmidt, Mendelsohn's sketches find the essence by deforming the intended building into a series of strong horizontals. Not necessarily a conscious reference, the two architects resolved visualizing a distinct feature with *like* sketches. To display the essence of either ribbon windows or horizontal ramps, they each chose a technique most able to convey the idea with a pointed medium. Pulling forward the most distinguishing feature became the edges. Here Schmidt was not creating a monster by recombining elements psychologically, but is exaggerating specific elements to make a caricature which is purely visual.

The great architect Santiago Calatrava's sketch for the Planetarium at the Valencia Science Centre references work by another architect and additionally evokes a metaphor. This sketch (Figure 4.11), from 1992, suggests a section drawing from the design for Newton's Cenotaph by Etienne-Louis Boullée. The building type of a planetarium requires a spherical shape and Boullée's Cenotaph, although a markedly different building type, was also conceived as an artificial sky. The final construction of this planetarium by Calatrava has been embedded in the Science Center, whose shape brings to mind a blinking eyelid. The metaphor of an eye was certainly intentional in the design. The suggestion of an eye, as the window to the soul, implies a search for knowledge and the learning that takes place in a science center. It appears Calatrava first sketched the circular form and then rendered it with watercolor. The nature of watercolor may be the best medium to reveal the internal concave form of the Planetarium. The drawing, as a representation of the future building, also elicits an atmospheric softness appropriate for studying the stars. Although Boullée's proposal was freestanding and significantly different from the design by Calatrava, a first glance sparks a memory.

FIGURE 4.11   Santiago Calatrava; Planetarium at the Valencia Science Centre.

Sketches are capable of conveying visual compilations that defy nature, such as unusual combinations that do not necessitate the logic of the connections. In a similar way, the exaggeration of specific features helps architects to understand particular aspects of immediate focus in their design process. The concentration may involve solving a specific problem, such as a detail, view or question of form. Exaggeration may assist to study an element more intently. As seen above, Morten Schmidt focused on the space between the two curved walls and the relative perforation of these walls, thus his immediate concern was not structure or dimensions. Architects through history, such as Hugh Ferriss, have used sketches to demonstrate conceptual notions of the building's presence in the context of a city. By the use of dramatic lighting, Ferriss exaggerated the height of a building to elicit a fantastical, and often inspirational, impression. The Italian Futurist architect Sant'Elia evoked a technological future in his dramatic sketches and, in a similar way, Cesar Pelli employed his sketch (Figure 3.13) to visualize the Petronas Twin Towers in the light of the Malaysian atmosphere.

This page of sketches by the Chicago architect Helmut Jahn (Figure 4.12) considers a high rise building in the context of a city. Helmut Jahn is the design principal of Murphy/Jahn. Their work has received many AIA Chicago Chapter awards, several Structural Engineering awards, and a national AIA award. A large and prolific firm, a few of their more recent projects include the Shanghai International Expo Center; FKB Airport Cologne/Bonn; the European Union Headquarters in Brussels; and the IIT Student Housing in Chicago.

This densely rendered page is a study for the 362 West Street building in Durban, South Africa. This analysis sketch carefully explores the building's footprint on the site with figure/ground diagrams. On this page, Jahn investigates three variations for the building across the top of the page. The second row of sketches examines several additional variations on the octagonal-shaped first option. These systematically presented sketches are beautiful in their record of a thought process,

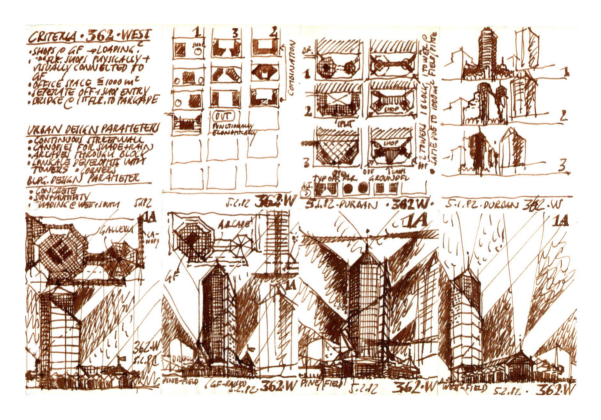

FIGURE 4.12   Helmut Jahn; 362 West Street Building, Durban, South Africa.

starting with the plan and immediately considering the three-dimensional manifestation. The four sketches on the lower half of the sheet envision the skyscraper at night, either lit from within or from its position in the city. In each instance, the background is not clouds, but rather a searchlight or directional streams of light emitting from behind the building. Plans and sections have been added onto these drawings to help understand the perspective view. Since the interior spaces in a high rise building are often designated by the tenants, Jahn was concentrating on the contextual presence so important to a skyscraper. The dramatic background anticipated the monumentality that is truly the function of a tall building. This caricature, or exaggeration, creating a theatrical view anticipates the monumentality of the future building.

In this sketch by Erich Mendelsohn (Figure 4.13) he uses many different indicators to help convey scale. Although often rendering sleek, machine-like buildings, Mendelsohn employs brief

FIGURE 4.13   Erich Mendelsohn; Hadassah University Medical Center, Mount Scopus, Jerusalem (graphite and colored pencil on tracing paper).

and abstract lines to render context and background. On this page of sketches for the Hadassah University Medical Center at Mount Scopus in Jerusalem, he uses window patterning and proportional form to describe scale. The sheet contains five images placed in close proximity. The top is an elevation with dark ribbon windows, very representative of his previous architectural work. The lower four sketches show a combination of small punched and ribbon windows at the corners of the building. Counting the rows of windows makes it possible to imagine the size and scale of the project.

It appears that the building sits on the crest of a hill, since the perspective looks up to the structure. This perspective renders a dramatic and monumental view. Because the buildings have been drawn with more detail than the context, and the context overlaps other buildings, it is conceivable that the large curved horizon lines were a later addition. It feels as if the arched sky was the last line to 'finish' the sketch and give it context. This large arc appears to indicate the illusion was complete and thus one unified entity. Similarly, the looped and scalloped lines in the foreground appear to represent trees and bushes. They have been drawn very quickly and seem to be used to 'frame' the perspective. It is remarkable that one rapid modulated line can demonstrate the siting of the building. Not taking the time to draw foliage, Mendelsohn caricatures the natural elements on the site with less articulation than the objects of his focus.

Morten Schmidt of schmidt hammer lassen renders human figures with the same contextual regard as Mendelsohn does foliage. In Figure 4.14 the people are no more than vertical lines. The ability to recognize them as humans stems from their relative size and placement on the walkways. They may be viewed as part of the context, and thus are indicators of scale, and with such a minimal and quick sketch they are sufficiently rendered as thick lines. This brilliantly quick and precise sketch exhibits the procession to the entrance of the Aarhus Museum of Modern Art,

FIGURE 4.14   Morten Schmidt; Aarhus Museum of Modern Art, ARoS.

ARoS. Here it appears the sketch was drawn with the processional layering of the walkway in mind. Interestingly, the trees showing void were outlined before the horizontal stripes of the building behind. If Schmidt was thinking only of the building, the trees would have been an afterthought. In the same way the entrance ramp was a priority and completed early. This sketch shows great skill. Schmidt's control of the medium is remarkable since the horizontal lines on the side of the building are nearly straight and parallel. The caricature of the zigzag lines to indicate the interior of the slice and the shadows in the trees, the minimal people, and using no superfluous lines provided him with an understanding necessary to make a judgment.

As another aspect of caricature, the human body becomes a metaphor for some architects in their sketches. Historically, caricature began with transforming the image of a human to visually reveal character traits. This comparison, of human features to qualities as abstract as personality, acts metaphorically to expose another dimension of understanding. Returning to Filarete's description of a building as a human being adds to the metaphorical comparison.

This sketch by Michael Rotondi (Figure 4.15), principal of RoTo Architects, which explores the organizational design for the Architecture and Art building at Prairie View A&M University, began as a metaphor of the human body. This plan displays a rectangle representing the organization of the building. The shape has been colored with yellow pencil and contains several wavy lines (one in red pencil). The words are most important on this sketch: to the left has been written 'memory' and 'meaning'; to the right Rotondi has written 'making'. Underneath the drawing he has added the words 'LABS', 'BODY', and 'The organization'.

It is clear he viewed the body metaphor in this project, as he has marked the left side of the drawing as the 'head'. Although the project in plan does not resemble a human form in any way, he was seeing the memory/meaning/cultural archives as the 'head'. The other parts placed along a spine add to the metaphor. On the rectangle, he also revealed the types of spaces and the potential materials for construction, things that are difficult to express visually in a diagram. The diagram, then, becomes part of his thinking from the conceptual metaphor to the anticipation of materials. It may have acted as a *parti*, which he returned to during the entire design process.

This sketch, with its simplicity, poignant wit and allusion to a truth, may be likened to a caricature, as it gave Rotondi the essence of the project. Kris and Gombrich provide insight into the connection between these sketches and the finished building when they note that '…caricature, showing more of the essential, is truer than reality itself' (Kris & Gombrich, 1938: 321).

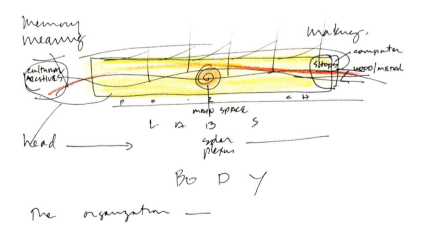

FIGURE 4.15   Michael Rotondi; PVAMU Head to Body. 'Prairie View A&M University, School of Art + Architecture, 2002'.

FIGURE 4.16   Santiago Calatrava; Human/Structure sketches.

Santiago Calatrava suggests anthropomorphic form in his architecture. He understands structural properties of materials through the physiology of animals and humans, and also their analogous shapes. In this sketch (Figure 4.16) Calatrava was equating a structural detail to a human form. This study is particularly interesting since he visually morphed the human into the steel form in a series of sketches. The left image reveals an elongated figure. The other three represent figures in various forms of abstraction, bent and outstretched as if reaching. The four sketches sit on a datum line that almost appears to be a ledge. The lines, describing the people, are fragmented, while smooth fluid marks replicate the characteristics of steel. The figures presented in profile flex where a human's torso meets the legs, finding the natural pose of a figure and also comparing the thickness of the steel to the thickness of a body. The addition of watercolor over the lines bestows a three-dimensional and muscular quality to both the human and the steel section. The figures exist in isolation; they have not been attached to the pieces they are intended to support. This detachment reinforces their autonomy as distinctly human. Identifying human forms to be molded into steel appears anthropomorphic in his work, since he compares human proportions and anatomic composition to stresses and the inanimate attributes of steel.

The Chicago Tribune Competition of 1922 provides some interesting examples of caricature in building proposals. All buildings, especially those imitating and distorting antiquity, caricature existing buildings in some way. *Architecture, Mysticism and Myth*, by William Lethaby, discusses how each building is in some way a representation of a tree, the first assemblage of shelter (Lethaby, 1974). Possibly then, it can be said that every building is a caricature; but a caricature relies upon

FIGURE 4.17   Frank Fort; Chicago Tribune Tower Competition, Entry 90.

representation. The caricature requires reference to the original figure so that it can ridicule. In this way, sketches reflect the personality and hidden meaning of the original in order to envisage the caricature, just as the artist looks to the human model for a subject of ridicule.

The Chicago Tribune Tower Competition offers many examples of ridicule in caricature. An entry by Frank Fort (Figure 4.17) proposes a massive granite building with rows of Greek *diaphers*. On the top rests a replica of a Greek temple. This might be viewed as a caricature of a temple, but it is less so than other projects wearing Greek robes (Figure 4.18). The project by Fort is a copy of

FIGURE 4.18   Milnar, Chapman and Markes; Chicago Tribune Tower Competition,
Entry 54.

a Greek temple, which appears to be exact in ornamentation and proportion. The ridicule seems evident as it could be asked, 'Why a Greek temple placed on a skyscraper for the Chicago Tribune Newspaper in Chicago?'

Other projects in the Chicago Tribune Tower Competition are less blatant, and seem to be more typical caricatures. The caricature consists of references to elements of a Greek temple, but the transformation, not so subtly, has been used to encourage contemplation about the role of a Greek

FIGURE 4.19   William Berg; Chicago Tribune Tower Competition, Entry 121.

temple. Does the Chicago Tribune Corporation have the ritual or sacred qualities to be a place of religion like a temple? The architects may be ridiculing the notion of praying to the almighty gods of communication, since some entries are topped with Mercury, the god of swiftness and communication, a likely symbol for a newspaper. The architects may have been responding to the monumentality of this skyscraper in Chicago in comparison to the incredible longevity of some Greek temples.

The caricature appears striking where the Greek temple is topped by a ziggurat roof or an angel (Figure 4.19). Combining the ritual monuments of different cultures emphasizes the tie of this building (or this corporation) to lasting and important structures. Also, the building can then be related to the knowledge, development and importance of these historical societies. The Program of the Competition document states, 'It cannot be reiterated too emphatically that the primary objective of the Chicago Tribune in instituting this competition is to secure the design for a structure distinctive and imposing – the most beautiful office building in the world' (1923, 31). With this statement in mind it must be assumed that each architect created the most beautiful building possible. It is interesting to observe what these architects in 1922 saw as 'most beautiful'. The Greek temples, Gothic cathedrals and Egyptian details are not surprising, as the architects looked to find the most beautiful buildings in the world for models. The building becomes a caricature of what each architect believed was beautiful.

There are a few factors which might influence the caricatures of many of the entrants. The year 1906 was the time of a highly publicized international competition for a Palace of Peace at The Hague. The historian Spiro Kostof writes that 'the overwhelming majority, including the top winners, was blatantly historicist' (1985: 685). The influences of the previous 15 years, besides the Palace of Peace, include Unity Temple by Frank Lloyd Wright; sketches by Sant'Elia; Union Station in Washington D.C.; factories by Peter Behrens; and Notre Dame, in La Raincy, by Auguste Perret. Another influence was the '...powerful Beaux-Arts method that affected almost everyone, traditionalist and usurper, in matters of composition' (Kostof, 1985: 685). Changing times made ridicule easy and created a great variety of entries.

The huge column submitted by Adolf Loos (1870–1933), who worked in Vienna and was an anti-ornamentalist (Figure 4.20), seems a caricature of antiquity especially since it was designed in 1922, 12 years after his stark Modernist Steiner House. The column, with its perfect proportions and fluting, is less a caricature than the project by Mathew L. Freeman, whose building is quite large and starkly simple with plain pediments. His column-topped building (Figure 4.21) distorts the column by shortening it. This column is offered as useless for all but ornamentation, as it has no windows or openings. On the other hand, Loos' column has a simple stepped back base much more consistent with a column, and the building-column describes useful space with windows.

Freeman's competition entry ridicules the use of a column, attaching the column to the building in an uncertain connection. As with artists' caricatures discussed earlier, the method of drawing allows this connection without questions of how it could be accomplished. The half column arbitrarily placed on a building seems quite easy in a sketch. This incomplete column is transformed to serve a purpose distinct from the function of a column. The ridicule conveyed by topping a building with a classical column in a time of impending Modernism, the distortion of this feature, the strange juxtaposition in relation to the pediments, the column's uselessness, and the audacity of placing this building prominently in Chicago, all exemplify the ridicule in caricature. Baudelaire expresses this ridicule in his work on caricature, '...the comic is a mark of human dualism, a sense of superiority over the object of laughter and of inferiority relative to the absolute' (Hannoosh, 1992: 9).

It is necessary to discuss a few final projects which use architecture and architects of the past as models for 'the most beautiful office building in the world.' A project by Bliss and Faville shows a drawing which appears almost as a replica of an Italian Bell tower (Figure 4.22). Similarly, a project by Saverio Dioguardi (Figure 4.23) resembles an Arch of Triumph. These sketches are caricatures, although not at all subtle; in these instances, a building is taken from history and transformed into a skyscraper for Chicago.

The Italian Bell tower copies a bell tower, but as a skyscraper it makes few alterations. The function may be somewhat changed; the tower is attached to a building of typical skyscraper fenestration and the location is modified. The image of an original bell tower is not transformed; it remains strikingly literal. Why does the Chicago Tribune need a bell tower? To call the congregation to mass? How functional is the large arched doorway opening one floor off the street? Why does a saint stand at the corner of this building? The caricature is beautiful in its ridicule. The juxtaposition to the city of Chicago satirizes the role of this bell tower.

FIGURE 4.20   Adolf Loos; Chicago Tribune Tower Competition, Entry 196.

This discussion of caricature has referred to a time in history when the role of artists changed to allow their creative nature to transform and recombine. Kris and Gombrich view the skills of an artist to ridicule a subject: '[f]rom an imitator he became a creator, from a disciple of nature its master. The work of art was a vision born in his mind…Thus for the first time the sketch was held in high esteem as the most direct document of inspiration' (1938: 331). This employment of caricature by artists gives insight into architectural sketches.

FIGURE 4.21   Mathew L. Freeman; Chicago Tribune Tower Competition, Entry 162.

One key to sketching and caricature is imagination, whether a human trait or a product of divine inspiration. Michelangelo uses the term *Fantasia* to mean creative imagination, a vital aspect for the artist or architect (Summers 1981). Having discussed *fantasia* earlier, it seems necessary in conclusion to reiterate its importance. Caricature's distinctive characteristics are contingent upon the viewer's perception of a mental impression, and how that image provides for new thinking. It becomes possible to view the thinking process in sketches and particularly in the wit of caricature. The caricature helps the architect's creative imagination through visual recombination.

FIGURE 4.22   Bliss and Faville; Chicago Tribune Tower Competition, Entry 104.

The quickness, economy, imagination, wit, intelligence, and ridicule of caricature offer a method to interpret architectural sketches. Caricature, in most cases, acquires its foundation from what is known. The social and cultural aspects of architecture determine what is caricatured because the ridicule of one period in history is not necessarily understood in another. Times of great change in

FIGURE 4.23   Saverio Dioguardi; Chicago Tribune Tower Competition, Entry 248.

architecture, when the new replaces the old, often provide a stage for ridicule. Through recombination, deformation and transformation, architects look to their 'inner self' for creative inspiration, which plays an important role in caricature. This quote by Kris and Gombrich can also apply to architects:

The artist,' they claimed, 'is not an imitator of crude reality. He goes beyond reality in visualizing the 'ideas', the essence of things. Only the artistic genius has this gift of vision which enables him to open his mind to the idea of beauty and to realize it in the work of his hand. 'Invenzione', power of imagination, is considered the most noble of the artist's gifts (1938: 331–332).

The instances where the architect uses caricature to comment on other buildings, details, or the human body, are dependent upon representation. The sketch as a caricature refers to a known element in order to distort and exaggerate. This is true in all but one situation; the exception is exhibited when the sketch is a caricature of the finished work. In most cases the sketch is completed before the finished building, or even simultaneously. The caricature in this event precedes the eventual building and is reminiscent of the sketch by containing characteristic concepts.

Caricature becomes evident in architectural sketches in several ways. A detail can speak of a building's entirety. This detail, in sketch form, is a premonition of, or becomes a simplified sign of, the building as a whole. A sketch can recombine building elements from history to caricature structures designed by other architects. The sketches in this chapter utilize various components to simplify and incorporate visual images. Another form of caricature in architectural sketches involves the metaphor of the human body. This metaphor is extremely common in proportioning buildings throughout history, but here the body also becomes caricatured.

Ridicule is an important issue in caricature, along with transformation and deformation. This ridicule can involve satirical transformation or absurd juxtaposition. The caricature shows visually in the deformation or exaggeration used to transform the subject into the ridiculous, so that the truth may be perceived in the distortion. The study of architectural sketches viewed through caricature can reveal another dimension in the interpretation of architecture.

BIBLIOGRAPHY

(1923). *The International Competition for a New Administration Building for The Chicago Tribune MCMXXII.* The Tribune Company.

(1971). *The Compact Edition of the Oxford English Dictionary.* Oxford University Press.

Aristotle. (1936). *Minor Works* (translated by W.S. Hett). Harvard University Press.

Barasch, M. (1985). *Theories of Art, From Plato to Winckelmann.* New York University Press.

Baudelaire, C. (1995). *Painters of Modern Life.* Phaidon.

Branham, R.B. (2001). *Bakhtin and the Classics.* Northwestern University Press.

Brower, R.A. (1974). *Mirror on Mirror: Translation, Imitation, Parody.* Harvard University Press.

Calvino, I. (1988). *Six Memos for the Next Millennium.* Harvard University Press.

Dentith, S. (2000). *Parody.* Routledge.

Frascari, M. (1991). *Monsters of Architecture: Anthropomorphism in Architectural Theory.* Rowman and Littlefield.

Gombrich, E. and Kris, E. (1940). *Caricature.* King Penguin Books.

Hannoosh, M. (1992). *Baudelaire and Caricature.* Pennsylvania State University Press.

Harpham, G.G. (1982). *On the Grotesque; Strategies of Contradiction in Art and Literature.* Princeton University Press.

Highet, G. (1962). *The Indignant Eye; the Anatomy of Satire.* Princeton University Press.

Horn, M. (1980). *The World Encyclopedia of Cartoons.* Chelsea House Publishers.

Hulten, P. (1987). *The Arcimboldo Effect; Transformation of the Face from the 16th to 20th Century.* Abbeville.

Hutcheon, L. (1985). *A Theory of Parody.* Methuen.

Kostof, S. (1985). *A History of Architecture.* Oxford University Press.

Kris, E. (1934). The Psychology of Caricature. *The International Journal of Psycho-Analysis,* pp. 286–301.

Kris, E. and Gombrich, E. (1938). The Principles of Caricature. *British Journal of Medical Psychology,* 17, pp. 319–37.

Kris, E. and Kurz, O. (1979). *Legend, Myth, and Magic in the Image of the Artist.* Yale University Press.

Lethaby, W.R. (1974). *Architecture, Mysticism and Myth.* The Architectural Press.

Lynch, J.G.B. (1974). *A History of Caricature.* Gale Research.

Rose, M. (1993). *Parody: Ancient, Modern, and Post-Modern.* Cambridge University Press.

Shikes, R.E. (1969). *The Indignant Eye.* Beacon Press.

Solomonson, K. (2001). *The Chicago Tribune Tower Competition: Skyscraper Design and Cultural Change in the 1920s.* Cambridge University Press.

Summers, D. (1981). *Michelangelo and the Language of Art.* Princeton University Press.

Swain, S. and Boyes-Stones, G.R. (2007). *Seeing the Face; Seeing the Soul: Poleman's Physiognomy from Classical Antiquity to Medieval Islam.* Oxford University Press.

Tigerman, S. (1982). *Chicago Tribune Tower Competition and Late Entries.* Random House.

Wright, T. (1968). *A History of Caricature and Grotesque in Literature and Art* (introduction by Barasch, F.K.). Frederick Ungar Publishing.

Zevi, B. (1970). *Erich Mendelsohn Opera Completa.* Etas Kompass.

CHAPTER 5

THE GROTESQUE SKETCH

The grotesque, as an artistic and literary movement in existence since the sixteenth century, has characteristics in common with certain aspects of architectural sketches. The significance of sketches for architects is their importance for imagination and visualization, and the grotesque may provide a window to help view expression by architects in relation to their architecture.

Sketches in their brief, incomplete, notably unfinished and imprecise states may be comparable to the intermediary qualities of the grotesque. These sketches hover between the ability to convey known substances and helping to discover the unknown, and in their ambiguity they become visible in the grotesque as fragmented or jumbled.

As a thought process sketches are ambivalent; they can weave different meanings on numerous levels simultaneously and, consequently, as grotesque items they can provide multiple interpretations. As facilitators of the design process, sketches constitute a process of creativity and, thus, a medium of transition or progression. As a process they are personal in nature and can depict metamorphosis and rebirth for the architect, through humor, satire and paradox.

Like caricatures, which also ridicule, architectural sketches as grotesque employ exaggeration and deformation. Although the grotesque is similar to caricature, and at several times in history they were seen as synonymous, there are also numerous differences in meaning. Many of these distinctions will be discussed when defining the grotesque, but one issue stands out as most evident. Caricature, although psychological and dependent upon the knowledge of the beholder, is displayed uniquely in the visual. The humor, ridicule, exaggeration and deformation are understood because of the likeness to or recombination of elements from the appearance of the original. By contrast, the grotesque can be revealed through visual, literary or narrative means. One need not *see* the situation in order to comprehend grotesque elements because the grotesque does not need an image to convey its message.

This chapter contemplates some meanings of the grotesque in order to better understand and draw conclusions about architectural sketches. Using some architectural examples will bring the meaningful relationship between sketches and the grotesque to light. One architect whose work seems to epitomize numerous qualities of the grotesque is Giovanni Battista Piranesi; it is his *Carceri* etchings that will help to clarify this relationship. As Piranesi uses both the theme and the technique of the grotesque in the *Carceri*, these etchings greatly resemble sketches revealing the many meanings of the grotesque.

The message of the grotesque is difficult to define. Although possible to cite certain examples of the grotesque, rules for its application are somewhat elusive. Geoffrey Harpham writes '[i]t is historically demonstrable that no single quality is constant throughout the range of generally accepted grotesques' (1982: xviii). Observers can find characteristics which are usually present and look to accepted examples, such as ambivalence, transition or paradox, but each instance uniquely combines elements producing the grotesque. A part of this difficulty in definition derives from the grotesque's historically changing meaning.

A contemporary dictionary definition discloses some common usage of the word 'grotesque':

1. A kind of decorative painting or sculpture, consisting of representations of portions of human and animal forms, fantastically combined and interwoven with foliage and flowers. b) A work of art in this style. Chiefly figures or designs in grotesque; in popular language, figures or designs characterized by comic distortion or exaggeration.

2. A clown, buffoon, or merry andrew. In a wider sense, of designs or forms: characterized by distortion or unnatural combinations; fantastically extravagant; bizarre, quaint.

3. Ludicrous from incongruity; fantastically absurd.

4. To give a grotesque form or appearance to; to caricature, travesty.

(Oxford English Dictionary)

These definitions denote many accepted meanings and *Webster's Dictionary* adds three synonyms: atypical, eccentric and fantastic. Harpham, through study of literature and art, adds some not so common and less tangible explanations. A few were mentioned above and more will be discussed, such as the qualities of ambivalence, transition, paradox, and activities pertaining to the lower stratum.

As stated earlier, the grotesque is not necessarily dependent upon the act of seeing, and a study must be dotted with examples from literature, as well as those from the visual arts. Noted writers whose works contain elements of the grotesque include Dante, Shakespeare, Cervantes, Rabelais, Poe, Ruskin, Faulkner and, more recently, Truman Capote.

HISTORY OF THE GROTESQUE

As a foundation, a general history of the grotesque reveals its changing meanings. The earliest historical mention of grotesque was in reference to the Roman *Grottesche*. In the *Quattrocento*, the search of grottos for remnants of a glorious past in Rome exposed wall paintings pertaining to these designs (Barasch, 1971). They were given the label *Grottesche* after 1480, when they were first found (Harpham, 1982). Harpham describes these delicate images: '[they were] dainty, innocuous frescos decorating the wall of Nero's *Domus Aurea* or Golden Palace' (1982: 23).

Frances Barasch explains how the 'dainty' images were used as ornament, '[t]hese paintings were designed to please the fancy and the eye rather than to instruct the soul…The ornaments it designated were pleasing, strange, fantastic, and bizarre; the designs were symmetrical, delicate, and harmonious' (1971: 18, 24). They were purely decorative and were fashioned after leaves and fruit, distinctly reminiscent of manuscript illumination (Figure 5.1).

The name *Grottesche* stems from grotto, pertaining to underground caves, and this association with antiquity and archeology provides a dark side to the meaning of the grotesque from its beginning (Harpham, 1982; Barasch 1971). Contrary to the fantastical fragile plants, Harpham suggests a second meaning in the subterranean connection, as the '…*grotesque*, then, gathers into itself suggestions of the underground, of burial, of secrecy' (1982, 27).

The *Grottesche* became popular with architectural decorators in Italy. This 'fantastic style' moved quickly across Europe, as the word *Grottesche* appeared on a list of expenditures for decorating Fountainebleau between 1540 and 1566 (Harpham, 1982: 23). Giorgio Vasari uses the term *grotesque* in his book on High Renaissance painters, *Lives of the Artists*, and adds to the meaning slightly. He emphasizes that the grotesque's imaginative qualities speak of 'bizarre fantasies', 'beautiful and imaginative fantasies', and 'strange fancies'(Vasari, 1946). Vasari extends the meaning to describe a subjective new style, rather than specifically replication of the ancient wall paintings (1946). With his view, these artistic masters were in control of 'rule, order, proportion, design and manner' (Vasari, 1946: 185). Referencing great antiquities excavated from caverns helped these artists to acquire beauty in their art and reinforced this connection to the grotesque (Barasch, 1971).

The grotesque style of painting, often described as 'strange fantasy,' was in direct conflict with Leon Battista Alberti's humanist rules of invention, especially since he purported a Vitruvian view of mathematical harmony, purity, and simplicity (Alberti, 1988; Barasch, 1971).[1] In sixteenth-century

---

[1] Barasch writes that grotesques were irrational and subjective, and '…humanists, following a description in Vitruvius, discovered in it an attack on the ornate style in general and against grotesques in particular' (1971: 28).

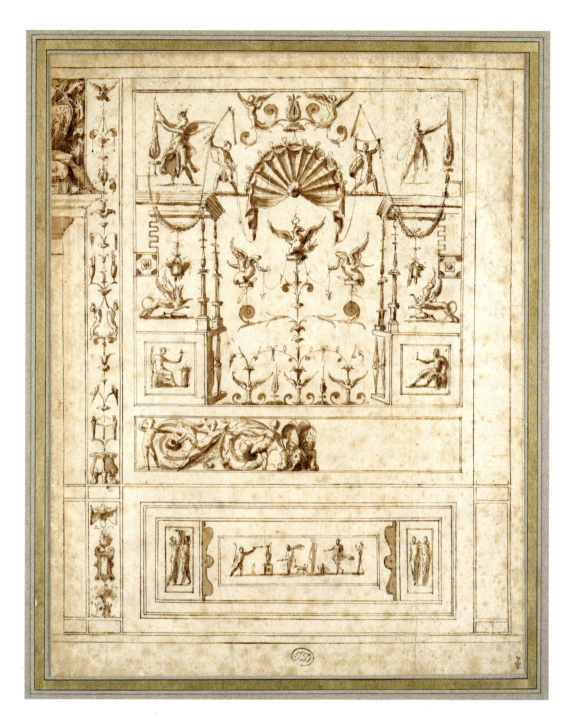

FIGURE 5.1   Perino del Vaga (Pietro Buonaccorsi); Design for a mural decoration
with grotesques for the Cagliostra of the Castel Sant' Angelo in Rome, c. 1544
(pen and brown ink on paper).

Italy, grotesques were considered 'manifestations of the decline of Roman art,' in all its decadence and
ornament; and, thus, in poor taste (Barasch, 1971). Although not necessarily labeled grotesque figures
when first completed, these profile sketches of people by Leonardo da Vinci (Figure 5.2) became

FIGURE 5.2   Leonardo da Vinci; Seven Studies of Grotesque Faces (red chalk on paper).

known as grotesque. Being possible examples of caricature and surely a search for the abnormal, they relate a story of the changing meaning of the grotesque. The quality of the grotesque as more real than real, or real to the extreme, is certainly evident in these sketches. Dwelling on the imperfect or distorted may be distinctly different from exaggeration, which is a way to locate character in caricatures. Here it is possible Leonardo was using sketches to revel in the variations of deformity found in human faces. For him, the fascination pertained to his empirical approach.

Barasch relates another change in the meaning of the grotesque:

> By the eighteenth century, the grotesque genre in ornamental art had become essentially French. Its name had been changed to arabesque by then, its origins in the antiquities were almost forgotten and the word 'grotesque' was reserved for other spheres of thought. (Barasch, 1971: 33)

The initially ornamental style of the grotesque took on new meaning set aside for gargoyles on cathedrals and the distorted illumination of manuscripts in the Middle Ages (Barasch, 1971). Wolfgang Kayser writes that the terms grotesque, arabesque and moresque were often used interchangeably before this split.

> The term 'moresque' is used to designate a kind of two-dimensional ornament exclusively composed of rigidly stylized leaves and tendrils painted over a uniform background which is preferably kept in black and white. The 'arabesque', on the other hand, involves the use of perspective; unlike the moresque, it is tectonic (that is, distinguishes between above and below); it is more profuse, so that the background is often completely hidden; and it avails itself of patterns composed of more realistic shoots, leaves, and blossoms, to which animal forms are occasionally added. (Kayser, 1963: 22).

These definitions of arabesque and moresque distinctly resemble grottesche wall painting. The underground, cavernous connotations of a grotto are strangely present in a new meaning of grotesque that includes terrifying ugliness, for example of gargoyles. In 1771, a German French dictionary, *Dictionnaire universal de la lanque francaise*, by Schmidlin, provides a definition: 'Figuratively speaking, grotesque means odd, unnatural, bizarre, strange, funny, ridiculous, caricatural, etc...' (Kayser, 1963: 28). Likewise in Germany, the grotesque was understood as having connotations of 'monstrous' (Barasch, 1971). In beginning to comprehend aspects of the grotesque as 'low comedy', sublime, and parody, defining concepts assists in exploring a more modern understanding.

From Germany, the *Traumwerk* style of painting was beautifully illustrated by the work of Pieter Brueghel the younger. His fanciful goblins and demons demonstrated Teutonic myth along with social comment (Barasch, 1971: 40). Wolfgang Kayser writes that the work of Pieter Brueghel the younger may be more true to a definition of the grotesque than paintings by the seemingly grotesque artist Hieronymus Bosch. '[Bosch] does not paint a Christian hell, whose monsters serve as God's tools in warning, tempting, or punishing, but an absurd nocturnal world of its own which permits of no rational or emotional explanation' (1963: 36).

Grotesques, denoted as 'chimera, demons, fools and clowns,' were called *antickes* in sixteenth-century England, and Barasch expresses the frivolous side of this issue:

> Antickes' in art were 'idle toyes' and not of 'any great use'... In addition 'antickes' came to be associated with Popery, and the Catholic Church was charged with using licentious ornamentation to lure and deceive its believers. English Protestants reasoned that 'anticks' were fantasies which perpetuated ancient superstition instead of expressing truth. (Barasch, 1971: 61)

About this time in England began a connection of grotesque to caricature. Nathan Bailey's *An Universal Etymological Dictionary* (1700) describes the grotesque, among other things, as something that is distorted (Barasch, 1971). Although caricature cannot be defined solely by distortion, because of its distinctive characteristics some caricature art was called *grotesque* (Barasch, 1971).

In addition to caricature, the grotesque became associated with 'ridiculous', 'burlesque' and 'farce', which strengthened connections to comedy and ridicule.

Until the nineteenth century, the meaning of the grotesque remained somewhat constant and was given less attention. Many individual artists could be considered as proponents of the grotesque even though an actual 'movement' had passed; they include Hogarth, Goya, Beardsley, and Munch, to name a few. A resurgence of interest in, and a redefinition of, the grotesque in art occurred in the early to mid-twentieth century with Surrealism.

As Vasari had viewed the grotesque as a subjective new style, Andre Breton also attacked logic and rationalism in his writing on the Surrealist movement. He advocated a separation from the limitations of modern culture (Kayser, 1963). Several of these painters found inspiration in the writings of Freud (Dali and Dreams) and Jung's 'collective unconscious', and consequently many evoked questions of the grotesque, such as De Chirico, Max Ernst and Ives Tanguy (Kayser, 1963: 169).

In contemporary definitions, Harpham writes that the grotesque deals with things beyond the 'real', not the real but the super-real.[2] '[The grotesque is] properly something more than the truth, something real in the extreme, not something arbitrary, false, absurd, and contrary to reality' (1982: xix, 131). Although the grotesque may have, at one time, meant the unreal, the real and grotesque have a unique commonality. John Ruskin implied this in his book *The Stones of Venice*:' [t]he grotesque sometimes gave "evidence of deep insight into nature"' (Harpham, 1982: xix). In comparison to this added dimension of the term, Harpham describes the grotesque as always present, especially in conjunction with supposed reality; he writes:

> *A recent book, on* The Grotesque in Photography, *completes this progression, displaying not only artificially distorted or rearranged images, but also technically uncomplicated photographs of hangings, murder victims, Che Guevara's staring corpse, and the famous picture, almost a modern icon, of the televised pistol execution of a Viet Cong. (Harpham, 1982: xix)*

The Surrealist painter, Giorgio de Chirico, suggests another reality of our modern world to express the grotesque, namely the machine. His stark streets and mechanically jointed mannequins fashion a '... fusion of realms, the mixture of organic and mechanical elements, which destroys the familiar order of our world view' (Kayser, 1963: 170). Paintings by de Chirico are substantially complex, but on a basic level his images acknowledge their historical counterparts; machines as demonically destructive (Kayser, 1963):

> *The mechanical object is alienated by being brought to life, the human being by being deprived of it. Among the most persistent motifs of the grotesque we find human bodies reduced to puppets, marionettes, and automata, and their faces frozen into masks. (Kayser, 1963: 183)*

GROTESQUE SKETCHES

The mechanical quality of the grotesque can be evidenced in the work of Giovanni Battista Piranesi. His *Carceri* etchings exhibit some of the more common, and a few of the little known, aspects of the grotesque in architectural sketches. Piranesi (1720–1778) engraved imaginative reconstructions of ancient Rome providing a hypothetical view of antiquity. Piranesi's *Carceri* etchings may be compared to architectural sketches since these etchings contain quick, expressive, and fantastic qualities, resembling a definition of architectural sketches. They are also grotesque because,

---

[2] This definition is reminiscent of Baudrillard's concept of the *hyper-real*: Baudrillard, J. (1983). *Simulations*. Semiotext.

in their visual presentation, they contain characteristics of accepted definitions of the grotesque; they are fanciful, bizarre, comically incongruous or absurd, ridiculously ugly, or depart markedly from the natural. These architectural etchings can be viewed as grotesque by virtue of their interpretive qualities. Some of the elements include transition (process or progression), ambivalence, fragmentation, deformation, their intermediary aspects, paradox and the grotesque's affinity for the lower stratum. As in caricature, the transformation and ridicule encourage comprehension of a truth beneath outward appearances.

Piranesi's work sublimely represents the grotesque, partially because of the obvious visual connections to traditional definitions of the grotesque, and also because of more complex notions of the grotesque that involve interpretation. These etchings provide comparison to sketches since they comprise characteristics typical of architectural sketches. They employ light expressive lines that are quick, vague, and often lacking in details. As do sketches, they represent the uncertain, changing, constantly transforming and tenuous stage of the design process. As described in earlier chapters, sketches often contain vague connections, and fantasy qualities. Piranesi's etchings present many of these traits, and can be described as having a vitality reminiscent of sketches.

For the *Carceri*, Piranesi used etching rather than engraving, presumably because it allowed him to work quickly and render expressive variations of lines.[3] Engraving being more labor intensive is a less spontaneous process. Although both provide the artist with the ability to produce a multitude of identical prints, etching promotes playful, quick lines. Similarly, architects use sketches to outline an abstract concept, then rework that same sketch until it becomes more detailed and definite.

Piranesi's *Carceri* suggest he was practicing a similar process, as evidenced by the several stages of the *Carceri* 'sketchings'. The etchings were published in a first state and then reworked to produce a second state that was distributed later. The technique seems to have suited Piranesi well, as he used what Werner Oechslin describes as quickness: '[t]he sketch is ideally suited for capturing the fleetingness of an idea' (1982: 103).

This method of etching/sketching, in comparison to drawing, allows the architect to find allusions and analogies during the action of drawing. E.H. Gombrich writes about how Leonardo used sketches for inspiration: '[h]e goes so far as to advise the artist to avoid the traditional method of meticulous drawing because a rapid and untidy sketch may in its turn suggest new possibilities to the artist' (1969, 189).

Piranesi completed ink sketches and drawings of the *Carceri* approximately coinciding with the *Carceri* etchings. Some of these sketches seem to resemble, or could have been preparation for, the etchings. Although these sketches appear similar they do not necessarily contain a pattern likeness to be preliminary for specific *Carceri* etchings. Piranesi revealed the looseness and innovation of his sketchy style when defending his imaginative creations from attack by his critics; he proclaimed '[t]hey despise my originality, I their timidity' (MacDonald, 1979: 29). Philip Hofer has noted Piranesi's quick expressive fantasies by stating that, '[h]is etching is as he intended it to be, almost freehand drawing seemingly made in a passionate hurry' (Hofer, 1973: xii). With these elements in mind, comprehending Piranesi's *Carceri* etchings as sketches becomes possible.

Many aspects of the *Carceri* etchings anticipate interpretive, polemical, recombining, analogical, ambiguous, or unstable elements of the grotesque.

Grotesqueries…stand at a margin of consciousness between the known and the unknown, the perceived and the unperceived, calling into question the adequacy of our ways of organizing the world, of dividing the continuum of experience into knowable particles. (Harpham, 1982: 3)

---

[3] With etching, Piranesi is able to work quickly, as the image is first scratched into wax, and then a process of acid bites the lines into the plate. The wax, being softer, allows fast motion as does a sketch. Engraving requires scratching into the plate, which is more labor intensive and slower, as the marks need to be deep enough to hold ink and thus print.

One quality of the grotesque implying 'elusive' is that of ambivalence. The concept of *ambiguity* exemplifies attributes distinctive of Piranesi's *Carceri*. The spaces are uncertain or indefinite in their endless depth, since walls and stairs fade into the distance or disappear in fog. Harpham explains these difficulties in understanding the shape of some objects or their connections to other things within the space. 'Within the gap of ambivalence or ambiguity, energy is confused, incoherent' (1982: 8).

Looking to Plate III (Figure 5.3) the location appears to be a large interior underground stone space, but on closer observation the ambiguities within this space are evident. The light appears to be emanating from the right, casting shadows to the left, but it is not streaming from grates above as might be expected in an underground space. The mutually conflicting possibilities express the ambivalence of the grotesque. The lighting summons a mysterious uncertainty between above ground and underground, and additionally between exterior and interior, as the shadows seem consistent with those made by direct sunlight (Tafuri, 1987).

The ambiguous properties of the sketches reinforce this dichotomy of interior and exterior, and the technique using undefined connections directly relates these sketches to the grotesque. Harpham writes of the paradox of inside and outside revealing '... the ambivalent is that which belongs to more than one domain at a time...[and] makes the grotesque image fluctuate in meaning' (1982: 4).

Piranesi alters the perspective point within these etchings so that the immediate space seems to continue rather than recede. When he wants space to recede he leaves the area light or undefined (his famous fog or steam). Manfredo Tafuri describes this space when analyzing Plate IX (Figure 5.4); he feels that the solid monument seems to melt into a huge elliptical arch, whose center quickly dissolves into empty space (1987: 26). For Tafuri this space describes the infinite and gives the plate a central lightness. This infinite space could express hope or an undefined future.

The polemic between exterior and interior spaces of which Tafuri writes is graphically achieved through techniques of perspective and illumination. The haunting of the space through these illusionary devices purposefully induces a feeling of the outside from the inside. It is possible Piranesi was questioning the political state by revealing the inside out. The more undefined the sketches, the greater our ability to read opposing meanings into them, since '[c]onfused things rouse the mind to new inventions' (Harpham, 1982: 146). Although undefined images allow imagination to interpret, it may be difficult to demarcate a boundary where maximum confusion leads only to chaos. Referring to play might impose some boundaries.

Tafuri feels Piranesi plays with his etchings as political statements, since his prisons contain torture devices and huddled people often in despair.[4] In the mechanics of torture, Piranesi perceives the bourgeois as advocating a '... corrosive, diabolical...[and] an anti-human element' (Tafuri, 1987: 31). He used the gloomy settings and symbolism to advance an assertion, one that was most likely not comprehended by most of his audience. He employed the strange fantasies as a medium with which to express this polemic, and these complex fantasies deceived his hidden meaning. Manfredo Tafuri describes the 'negative utopia' of the *Carceri*: '... Piranesi merely exalts the capacity of the imagination to create *models*, valid in the future as new values, and in the present as immediate contestations of the "abuse of those who possess wealth, and who make us believe that they themselves are able to control the operations of Architecture"' (1987: 29).

Some of the delusion resides in the immense, and out of scale, mazes of the underground fantasies. Another part lies in the broken bodies of the forlorn inhabitants, which depict the common population dominated by the bourgeoisie. These perfects of the future present contradictions (Tafuri, 1987: 29). John Wilton-Ely describes the '... bridges, balconies, etc...[as] a nervous continuum with no point of stability or rest throughout' (1978: 83).

---

[4] Piranesi was born in 1720, and although his travel was mostly confined to Italy, he must have been aware of the many conditions which sparked the French Revolution, and the decadence of the Imperial Age and the Baroque.

FIGURE 5.3   Giovanni Battista Piranesi; *Carceri*, Plate III. A vaulted building with a staircase leading round a central column with barred window in the centre. 1760s.

FIGURE 5.4   Giovanni Battista Piranesi; *Carceri*, Plate IX. A prison door surmounted by
a colossal wheel-shaped opening crossed by beams. 1760s.

With the altered perspective, Piranesi sets observers in a tenuous position, forcing them to feel off balance in this continuous space. This is partially evidenced by the vacillation between 'center' or 'place', and this unnerving instability presents a visual message that supports this view (Tafuri, 1987: 27).

Piranesi's depiction of the domination of common people reveals a 'reign of the most absolute coercion' (Tafuri, 1987: 31). Here, he is not eluding to a specific condition to create a new reality. He is, instead, presenting his version of a perceived or exaggerated image to express his political view. The delusion of truth in these etchings shows domination of mankind. This torture and humiliation is the 'active decomposition' of the status quo (Tafuri, 1987: 37). In keeping with Rousseau, Piranesi sees the 'chaos of the city' as an 'equation between city and nature' (Tafuri, 1987: 36).

Piranesi was deceptive with buildings, or prisons, that do not exist. He controlled the visual space by making a fictitious environment since he was describing a loss of freedom. It may have been a controlling mechanism to make the observer feel uneasy and thus understand the 'decomposition'. John Wilton-Ely reinforces Tafuri's suggestion by proposing that '... the *Carceri* reveal the processes of a highly controlled discipline, exploiting to an unprecedented degree Baroque illusionist devices of perspective and lighting' (1978: 81).

These illusionist devices are reminiscent of caricature, in that Piranesi leaves the connections vague (Wilton-Ely, 1978: 19). He uses construction methods, common for his time, but does not detail any connections, leaving the observer to project the actuality. In a caricature, it is unnecessary to question the combination of a human and an inanimate object, for example, and this may also be true of the sketchy style that Piranesi used. Employing unusual lighting diminishes areas into vagueness that he wanted to de-emphasize.

In *Carceri* Plate XII (Figure 5.5) the shadows are cast diagonally to the left at approximately 45 degrees. Contrarily, the lightest area, the origin of the illumination, appears to be the lower right corner of the etching. Piranesi was deceptive to his liking to create a controlled atmosphere.[5] He provides sufficient two-dimensional illusion in his prisons for the viewer to wonder about its existence (MacDonald, 1979). The *Carceri* contain enough vagueness and freedom to speak of possibilities and to question the norm set forth by Baroque artists and architects.

The action of *possibilizing* brings to the surface another important aspect of the grotesque that is discussed by Harpham and can be seen in sketches: the role of transition and the intermediary.

> *[T]he grotesque is embodied in an act of transition, of metonymy becoming metaphor, of the margin swapping places with the center. It is embodied in a transformation of duality into unity, of the meaningless into the meaningful. And all these discoveries were available right at the start: they were the very first things revealed about the grotesque, and they remain its primary features. (Harpham, 1982: 16)*

Piranesi's *Carceri* Plate VII (Figure 5.6) elegantly expresses a 'process or progression' of transition. On a basic or formal level, it is possible to view this etching in terms of movement since the many layers of balconies force the observer's eyes to explore the depth of this etching. The stairs and balconies (the subject matter) speak of progression and, consequently, these stairs move diagonally and vertically through the space as a theme. This movement appears to oscillate between the two dominant vertical columns. The composition of the balconies moves diagonally up, right to left, and the spiral stairs swing diagonally down, left to right, as a counter balance. Similarly the large cable swings to the right and has been echoed by an arch breaking to the left. The strong rhythm

---

[5] Manfredo Tafuri names Piranesi the 'wicked architect'. He quotes Klossowski describing a 'worthy' philosopher. It is the wicked man that favors his strongest passion, but the 'greater evil lies in concealing the passion under the appearance of thought, the wicked one sees nothing in the thought of the honest man than the covering up of an impotent passion'. He writes that in concealing the passion lies a great evil, but that of describing an action rather than committing it. He concludes that drawing, but not building, is wicked for an architect. Piranesi is only known to have completed one building (1987: 46–47).

FIGURE 5.5   Giovanni Battista Piranesi; *Carceri*, Plate XII. An arched chamber
with lower arches surmounted by posts and chains, with strong light entering from the
right-hand side. 1760s.

of vertical railings reinforces a repetitious pattern, acting as a sequence of events. In the same way, Piranesi draws cables not in a thicker line to be more dominant but with many parallel lines that give the etching a fluctuating, nervous quality.

On a level beyond that of the obvious formal composition, there is potential to find elements of transition, and additionally of the intermediary. The people in the space move with undetermined action as if they are prisoners, but they have unusual freedom to wander this labyrinthine space. In the first state of this etching, several of the people are partially distorted by steam. Others seem to have weapons (vertical lines behind them), and still others are huddled, possibly helping each other walk. The function of this dismal space is indeterminate, which leads it directly into the grotesque.

The 'fragmented and jumbled' messages evoke the intermediary, and thus the meaning hovers between the known and the unknown: things that are knowable and those that require interpretation (Harpham, 1982). Harpham reveals another aspect – the grotesque acts as a mediator between our knowledge and ambiguity. 'Resisting closure, the grotesque object impales us on the present moment, emptying the past and forestalling the future' (1982: 16). An observer of the etchings may not be completely confident of Piranesi's meaning; he might be commenting on a desperate situation, with the etching as an agent of political criticism. This prison might represent a view of a bleak future. The grotesque is within this gap of ambiguity; it is '...dynamic and unpredictable, a scene of transformation or metamorphosis.' (Harpham, 1982: 8)

FIGURE 5.6   Giovanni Battista Piranesi; *Carceri*, Plate VII. An immense interior, with numerous wooden galleries, and a drawbridge in the centre. 1760s.

Harpham describes this mode of transformation, an interval of the grotesque, as similar to a paradigm crisis (1982: 17). This transformation might be a medium with which to find the truth through absurdity and exaggeration, since it may be necessary to reside in the interval of the grotesque to find radical insight (Harpham, 1982: 46).

In the lower center of this etching (Figure 5.6) two unstructured images can be seen coming out of the mist; they seem to be two dark crosses in this seemingly Godless place. This is a strange contradiction to the chains of confinement or disparity. Piranesi might be exposing the mid-region between a metaphysical heaven or hell (Harpham, 1982: 8). Again, as Harpham expresses, the grotesque can be seen as an ' ... intertextual "interval" ... [when] looking for unity between center and margin, the interpreter must, whether he finds it or not, pass through the grotesque' (1982, 38).

The grotesque then, acts as a means of emerging understanding, which is the process of 'making and unmaking meaning' (Harpham, 1982: 40). As established, the etchings in their quickness and incompleteness can be viewed as sketches, in that they have an unfinished quality. This is particularly evident as Piranesi published them in one state and reworked them to be distributed again. They are part of a creative process; a short pause within a passage of a larger story. Each of the *Carceri* has the same theme and could be seen as a piece within a series. This is still another example of these sketches as grotesque, where they exhibit a combination of transition and the medium of the intermediary. These qualities are well stated in a quote from George Santayana:

> *If this confusion is absolute, the object is simply null; it does not exist aesthetically, except by virtue of materials. But if the confusion is not absolute, and we have an inkling of the unity and character in the midst of the strangeness of the form, then we have the grotesque. It is the half-formed, the perplexed and the suggestively monstrous. (Santayana, 1961: 175)*

Again, in Figure 5.6, it is confusing to view strange forms that are ambiguous but also resemble the grotesque in their relationship to the human body. The turret on the right is disturbing because, when glancing away, it has a bizarre resemblance to a face. The shape can allow perception of various forms, as it is incomplete enough to permit interpretation. William MacDonald notices the bollard in these prisons (especially Figure 5.7), a symbol for authority, and writes: '[a]t times they become almost anthropomorphic and rather threatening, ... where the forms resemble humanoids ...' (MacDonald, 1979: 14). These abstract body forms seem to function as an analogy in which the workings of a prison are compared to the human body.

The human body is vital to understanding the grotesque and, with this in mind, Mikhail Bakhtin acquaints the reader with the medieval world of Rabelais (1968). Degradation and bodily functions reveal a transformation important to the grotesque. For life in this time, the carnival was the midzone between mere existence and art (Bakhtin, 1968). The Middle Ages was a time of festival and carnival, as people gathered to mark time and celebrate life. All that was sacred was put aside for gay parodies and festivities: '... the carnival-grotesque form exercises ... to consecrate inventive freedom, to permit the combination of a variety of different elements and their rapprochement, to liberate from the prevailing point of view of the world, from conventions and established truths, from clichés, from all that is humdrum and universally accepted' (Bakhtin, 1968: 34).

The festival allowed a new order of things, especially the parody of sacred texts and rites. With the 'feast of fools', drunkenness and freedom of laughter were permitted. 'The truth of laughter embraced and carried away everyone; nobody could resist it' (Bakhtin, 1968: 82). Laughter ceremonies paralleled official religious services and, subsequently, the 'feast of fools' allowed, for example, the grotesque degradation of various church rituals and symbols. It also provided for a transfer to the material bodily level, which involved gluttony and drunken orgies on the alter table, indecent gestures, and disrobing (Bakhtin, 1968). Bakhtin writes that the carnival involved the joyful laughter of celebration, but that it also revealed an escapist opportunity within a difficult life by lowering that which was held on high by society.

'The essential principle of grotesque realism is degradation, that is, the lowering of all that is high, spiritual, ideal, abstract; it is a transfer to the material level, to the sphere of earth and body

FIGURE 5.7   Giovanni Battista Piranesi; *Carceri*, Plate XIII. Colonnaded interior with a broad staircase divided in two by a stone projection with barred window. 1760s.

in their indissoluble unity' (Bakhtin 1968, 19). The fool could be king for a day, revered and honored by his drunken neighbors. An example of this occurs in Victor Hugo's *The Hunchback of Notre Dame* where Quasimodo is crowned and paraded through the streets. As rules broke down and roles reversed, people could be lewd and unmannered. 'Grotesque realism knows no other lower level; it is the fruitful earth and the womb. It is always conceiving' (Bakhtin, 1968: 21). The body that defecates and performs sexual intercourse reveals its humanness. Bakhtin continues: '[n]ot only parody in its narrow sense but all the other forms of grotesque realism degrade, bring down to earth, turn their subject into flesh' (1968: 20).

This contact with the earth also means rebirth; Rabelais expresses the lowest level of life, but returns it to the cycle of life (1928). 'The grotesque image reflects a phenomenon in transformation, an as yet unfinished metamorphosis of death and birth, growth and becoming' (Bakhtin, 1968: 24). It is this rebirth which provides a context within which to view the *Carceri* etchings. The seemingly contradictory principle of rebirth in the grotesque might be a theme here, as Piranesi is inviting a comprehension of another aspect of human nature by showing the lowest degradation of the human condition. The contact with the earth, as these underground spaces disclose, adds a new dimension of interpretation to Piranesi's choice of subject. It is possible the etchings represent a false face for a new life or hope from despair. Bakhtin prefers to choose hope:

Mask is connected with the joy of change and reincarnation, with gay relativity and with the merry negation of uniformity and similarity, it rejects conformity to oneself ... The mask is related to transition, metamorphoses, the violation of natural boundaries, to mockery and familiar nicknames. (Bakhtin, 1968: 39)

The joy of laughter and rebirth, common during the Middle Ages, revived and changed its meaning in pre-Romanticism and Romanticism. 'It became the expression of subjective, individualistic world outlook very different from the carnival folk concept of previous ages, although still containing some carnival elements' (Bakhtin, 1968: 36). As a secondary and slightly contrary argument, the Romantics viewed the grotesque differently. Coming near the end of the eighteenth century, the Romantic Period coincides with much of the time Piranesi was working, as the *Carceri* date somewhere between 1745 and 1760 (Hofer, 1973).

Laughter was also an important transformation of the Romantic grotesque, '…[but] laughter was cut down to cold humor, irony, sarcasm. It ceased to be joyful and triumphant hilarity. Its positive regenerating power was reduced to a minimum' (Bakhtin, 1968: 38). It is possible that Piranesi's *Carceri* describe a sarcastic pessimism more characteristic of the Romantics. Where Rabelais's devils are wonderful 'jovial fellows, or comic monsters', the Romantics dwell on the devil as 'terrifying melancholy and tragic' and see the grotesque as 'nocturnal and dark' (Bakhtin, 1968: 40–41).

It would be easy to describe the *Carceri* as 'nocturnal and dark,' except for the paradoxical omnipresent light. It is interesting that John Ruskin (1819–1900), in his book *The Stones of Venice*, possibly a hundred years after Piranesi (and Romanticism), calls the late Renaissance a 'grotesque' Renaissance and describes it as in the 'spirit of jesting' (Ruskin, 1907: III, 102). Here, after Romanticism, Ruskin was returning to a view of the grotesque as characterized by joyful laughter. This paradoxical juxtaposition of darkness and light in the grotesque is reiterated in Ruskin's light-hearted view:

This spirit of idiotic mockery is, as I have said, the most striking characteristic of the last period of the Renaissance, which, in consequence of the character thus imparted to its sculpture, I have called grotesque; but it must be our immediate task, and it will be a most interesting one, to distinguish between this base grotesqueness, and that magnificent condition of fantastic imagination, which was above noticed as one of the chief elements of the Northern Gothic mind. (Ruskin, 1907: 110–111)

Ruskin examines two conditions of mind that combine to describe the grotesque: kinds of jest and kinds of fearfulness (1907, 115: 127). These concepts are distinctly reminiscent of the seventeenth- and eighteenth-century concept of the sublime as beautiful terror. Ruskin does seem to agree with the more complex definition of the grotesque involving parody and interpretation. He writes about the 'noble' grotesque:

For the master of the noble grotesque knows the depth of all at which he seems to mock, and would feel it at another time, or feels it in a certain undercurrent of thought even while he jests with it; but the workman of the ignoble grotesque can feel and understand nothing, and mocks at all things with the laughter of the idiot and the cretin. (Ruskin, 1907: 128)

This dichotomy exemplifies another aspect of a definition of the grotesque – that of affinity versus antagonism (Harpham, 1982). Affinity suggests a resemblance or similarity, whereas antagonism expresses opposition or hostility. Kayser wrote that '[t]he grotesque is a structure. Its nature could be summed up in a phrase that has repeatedly suggested itself to us: THE GROTESQUE IS THE ESTRANGED WORLD' (1963: 184).

The removal from affections suggests intermediary qualities but it also contains elements of paradox, especially in pairings of 'high' and 'low'. The grotesque is the ideal versus the abnormal, as in pairs like the beauty and the beast (Harpham 1982). Harpham describes the importance of this intermediary dichotomy characteristic of the grotesque: '[i]f the grotesque can be compared to anything, it is to paradox' (1982: 19).

The fact that the *Carceri* etchings can be considered sketches makes room for interpretation and paradox, important elements for the grotesque. The scenes are fantastic and bizarre, since it would be unusual to have experienced spaces as large, complex, and endless as these. They are incongruous or absurd compared to most people's experience. They are often ugly in their dank, crumpled deterioration, and depart from a common definition of the natural.

Returning to the issue of light, it is possible to view incongruous or unnatural instances when studying the gratings of these underground spaces. *Carceri* Plates III, XII and XII (Figures 5.3, 5.5, 5.7) exhibit large barred openings supposedly leading to tunnels or other underground spaces. The gratings themselves are dark, and the space between the bars is lighter in value, which brings into question the paradox of a light exterior with the light source's origin a mystery. Part of this paradox lies in the factor of the sketch, since seeing the etching Plate XII (Figure 5.5) as a sketch reveals the importance of the technique of the line. Piranesi draws the positive objects with line, to reveal the shapes quickly. In his hurry to define the form, he does not draw the negative space to reveal the positive but draws the object itself. An artist with more time would draw the space between the bars dark. To interpret the role or function of the gratings suggests an encounter with a grotesque paradox created by the quickness and fervor of the sketch. Harpham's example applies to this etching:

> *The delight of interpretation is the puzzling-out of this truth, which is implied just as strongly by what is left out as by what is included. It is 'the gaps, left or overleaped by the haste of the imagination' that form the grotesque character; and the mind, which hates gaps as nature hates a vacuum, leaps to fill them in through interpretation to the point where the grotesqueness vanishes and the image appears, if not as 'Gospel' (as Ruskin said) at least as a compressed allegory. (Harpham, 1982: 19)*

Further, it is possible to comprehend in the etching defined or more detailed objects rendered with more and darker lines, independent of their distance from the observer. Shadows in the background are all the same gray regardless of their distance from the light, which encourages comprehension of the grotesque in the intermediary qualities of this sketch. The strange ambiguous shadows on the walls and figures in the foreground are fragmented and jumbled (Harpham, 1982: 18). They reside between the known and the unknown and, as allusions, support analogies to many known objects. Harpham explains, '[w]e can see that grotesque forms present great opportunities for the imaginative intellect, for they are pre-eminently interpretable' (1982: 19). These undefined forms sometimes seem to be shadows, at other times objects or figures; they command attention as the lines are shorter and more definite in length, in contrast to the long consistent lines given to other shadows. The long lines give similar texture to shadows both on rock and wood, a technique that gives consistency to the sketch and, in treating materials in a similar way, plays down the change in surfaces. This is another paradox created by the 'passionate hurry' of the sketching style.

What truth can Piranesi be stating with this incredible transformation? This fantastical space, on one level, prepares one for the wonders of a possible built environment. The huge depth, exaggerated scale, consistent lighting, and patterning of values, interpretively or metaphorically suggest spaces which Piranesi felt or experienced. Kayser writes that: 'THE GROTESQUE IS A PLAY WITH THE ABSURD' (1963: 187). Some of these spaces seem unreasonable or incongruous, which links them to absurdity, especially in light of their paradoxical inconsistencies. What can be viewed as absurd may be dependent upon individual interpretation. As with caricature, the viewer must have knowledge of the subject or be able to see more than what is obvious. This ability to observe more than the obvious figures in several examples of the grotesque in literary classics. Classic texts can be read and reread by many generations and are open to a variety of interpretations. They are timeless and, using Harpham's discussion of *Wuthering Heights* as an example, one finds issues of the grotesque such as indeterminacy, repetition, metamorphosis, the monstrous and interpretation:

> *The classic text is distinguished by its high level of significant indeterminacy; the repair of indeterminacy gives rise to the generation of meaning. Generations of readers die off, liberating the text from their necessarily culture-bound interpretations, and permitting later generations to explore and to repair other newly discovered lesions, or gaps of indeterminacy in the surface of meaning. (Harpham, 1982: 79)*

These are examples of the grotesque that may fit into a generational interpretation but also may be universal. Piranesi uses many of these elements, such as indeterminacy, repetition, metamorphosis and the monstrous. In comparison the process is similar; whether verbal or visual, the common ground is imaginative interpretation.

> *These are described by Nabakov in* Invitation to a Beheading *as absurd objects, shapeless, pockmarked, mottled, knobby things which when placed before a distorting mirror became handsome and sensible ... the* nonnons *could be said to stand for the text, or the artifact itself; the mirror is the act of interpretation. (Harpham, 1982: 21)*

The grotesque is also the mirror that helps differentiate, translate and understand the unknown. It assists in the viewing of multiple interpretations, not necessarily providing complete understanding, but providing an inkling of something more. The confusion lies in the uneven ground-plane and how the observer's eyes are kept constantly moving in and out of the spaces. This pattern of dark and light stripes gives the sketch a nervous quality, as one's eye can never rest.

> *Fragmented, jumbled, or corrupted representation leads us into the grotesque; and leads us out of it as well, generating the interpretive activity that seeks closure, either in the discovery of a novel form or in a metaphorical, analogical or allegorical explanation. (Harpham, 1982: 18)*

The rhythmic pattern of darks and lights makes the drawing consistent and yet exciting. Even the dark figures help unify the scene; they assist in understanding the scale as exaggerated and, being substantially darker, act as weights to hold down the perpetual space.

These architectural sketches transport their viewers to another place and time. They are excited about the possibilities, and each observer wants to arrive at his or her own conclusions as to whether this is an ancient, recently discovered ruin from some great age of architecture, or a place discovered in a new world.

The 1700s were a time of new travel, as trips abroad brought back fascinating examples of antiquity from Palmyra and Egypt, for example. Drawings such as these undoubtedly helped to excite an interest in archeology. It is possible to draw individual conclusions, but Piranesi with his theatrical design experience has supplied an interval – an analogy or transition – to support the adventure, which helps locate meaning in this environment. 'A fine grotesque,' Ruskin said, 'was the expression, in a moment, by a series of symbols thrown together in a bold and fearless connection, of truths which it would have taken a long time to express in any verbal way' (Harpham, 1982: 19).

Piranesi's architectural sketches demonstrate the grotesque. The *Carceri* etchings can be compared to sketches in their loose and undefined techniques. 'Piranesi's etched lines dance and soar, stimulating the beholder's imagination at the same time that they fill him with wonder, a deep sadness and a sense of mystery' (Hofer, 1973: xii). His etchings/sketches are grotesque in their use of technique, in that the lines describing both positive and negative space are paradoxical. The shadows show omnipresent light, leaving the space intermediary and confusing. The aspects of Piranesi's perspective, and uncertain spaces and shapes, convey undetermined interpretation.

The messages of Piranesi's *Carceri* also utilize concepts of the grotesque. The underground spaces speak of dank despair, which connects them to deformation, bodily degradation and the earth, and in turn communicates a metamorphosis of new life. Similarly, Piranesi's light, which is undetermined and omnipresent, expresses, in ambivalence, the paradox of the grotesque. There is also a theme of social comment that is revealed in transition and paradox. Piranesi, himself, reveals the grotesque, as Tafuri calls him the 'wicked architect' because his arguments are made solely with drawings rather than buildings. Even the technique of redrawing the *Carceri*, each time a redefinition, provides a transition and progression, each a rebirth.

Historically, the definition of the grotesque is difficult. Its meaning has changed as its elements were interpreted differently. Kayser writes about the role of interpretation for the grotesque – that it is 'AN ATTEMPT TO INVOKE AND SUBDUE THE DEMONIC ASPECTS OF THE WORLD' (1963: 188). With the demons of the world in mind, it is conceivable to reiterate the main concepts of a modern definition of the grotesque: ambiguity, transition, deformation, aspects of the lower stratum, paradox and interpretation. Through these notions it is possible to view how the grotesque assists in understanding more about architectural sketches.

BIBLIOGRAPHY

1971. *The Compact Edition of the Oxford English Dictionary*. Oxford University Press.

Alberti, L.B. (1988). Translated by Rykwert, J., Leach, N. and Tavernor, R. *On the Art of Building in Ten Books*. MIT Press.

Arnold, D. and Ballantyne, A. (2004). *Architecture as Experience; Radical Changes in Spatial Practice*. Routledge.-

Bacou, R. (1975). *Piranesi Etchings and Drawings*. New York Graphic Society.

Bakhtin, M. (1968). *Rabelais and His World*. MIT.

Barasch, F.K. (1971). *The Grotesque; A Study in Meanings*. Mouton.

Baudrillard, J. (1983). *Simulations*. Semiotext.

Bloomer, J. (1993). *Architecture and the Text; Joyce and Piranesi*. Yale University Press.

Bosch, H. (2001). Hieronymus Bosch; the Complete Paintings and Drawings. Harry N. Abrams.

Bovey, A. (2002). *Monsters and Grotesques in Medieval Manuscripts*. University of Toronto Press.

Connelly, F. (2003). *Modern Art and the Grotesque*. Cambridge University Press.

Dudley, A. (1997). *The Image in Dispute; Art and Cinema in the Age of Photography*. University of Texas Press.

Fabricius, J. (1976). *Alchemy – The Medieval Alchemists and Their Royal Art*. Bagger International.

Gombrich, E.H. (1969). *Art and Illusion; A Study in the Psychology of Pictorial Representation*. Princeton University Press.

Harpham, G. (1982). *On the Grotesque; Strategies of Contradiction in Art and Literature*. Princeton University Press.

Hersey, G. (1988). *The Lost Meaning of Classical Architecture; Speculation on Ornament from Vitruvius to Venturi*. MIT.

Hofer, P. (1973). *Giovanni Battista Piranesi; The Complete First and Second States*. Dover.

Hyman, T. and Malbert, R. (2000). *Carnivalesque*. Hayward Gallery.

Kayser, W.J. (1963). *The Grotesque in Art and Literature*. Indiana University Press.

Kort, P. and Bergius, H. (2004). *Comic Grotesque; Wit and Mockery in German Art, 1870–1940*. Prestel.

MacDonald, W.L. (1979). *Piranesi's Carceri; Sources of Invention*. Smith College.

Maiorino, G. (1991). *The Portrait of Eccentricity; Arcimboldo and the Mannerist Grotesque*. Pennsylvania State University Press.

O'Conner, W. (1962). *The Grotesque; An American Genre*. Southern Illinois University Press.

Oechslin, W. (1982). The Well-Tempered Sketch. *Daidalos*, **5**, pp. 99–110.

Rabelais, F. (1928). *Gargantua and Pantagruel*. The Modern Library.

Regier, K.J. (1987). *The Spiritual Image in Modern Art*. Theosophical Publishing House.

Ruskin, J. (1907). *The Stones of Venice*. J.M. Dent.

Santayana, G. (1961). *The Sense of Beauty; Being the Outline of Aesthetic Theory*. Collier.

Scott, I.J. (1975). *Piranesi*. St. Martin's Press.

Sekler, P.M. (1962). *Notes on Old and Modern Drawings; Giovanni Battista Piranesi*. Enschedé.

Singleton, C.S. (1969). *Interpretation, Theory and Practice*. The John Hopkins Press.

Smiles, S. and Moser, S. (2005). *Envisioning the Past; Archaeology and the Image*. Blackwell.

Tafuri, M. (1987). *The Sphere and the Labyrinth; Avant-Gardes and Architecture From Piranesi to the 1970s*. MIT.

Trodd, C. and Barlow, P. (1999). *Victorian Culture and the Idea of the Grotesque*. Ashgate.

Vasari, G. (1946). *Lives of the Artists*. Simon and Schuster.

Wilton-Ely, J. (1978). *The Mind and Art of Giovanni Battista Piranesi*. Thames and Hudson.

Wilton-Ely, J. (1993). *Piranesi as Architect and Designer*. Yale University Press.

Wright, T. (1968). *A History of Caricature and Grotesque in Literature and Art*. Frederick Ungar.

Yourcenar, M. (1984). *The Dark Brain of Piranesi and other Essays*. Farrar, Straus, Giroux.

CHAPTER 6

OBSERVATION/COMPENDIUM AND *LIKENESS*

As stated earlier, and reinforced with examples in the various chapters, it is impossible to draw definitive conclusions concerning architectural sketches. Although sketches embody all that architects do, and thus are the medium for design, their fluctuating and intangible qualities enable 'possibilizing' activities. This study has presented a new view of architectural sketches, especially because little research has dealt with the theoretical issues beyond the 'how to' of sketching. Whether sketches are employed as a means to elicit initial inspiration or for assistance during the various stages of design, it is their revelatory nature that provides a deeper understanding beneath surface impressions. Sketches are both physical and intangible and, since they are also interpretive, they resist closure. Because their meanings undergo continual development, it is only possible to speculate about their shifting qualities.

This book has raised questions about architectural sketches, and has provided connections to known theories of play, caricature and the grotesque, but has avoided specific answers. The sketches themselves are compelling – they ask if there are limits to sketching, and what they may be. With this it is possible to question the nature of the dialogue between architects and their sketches. How can we better listen and learn from these sketches? What in them speaks to a thinking process? If all architects use sketches, why is it so difficult to define or explain them? To answer questions such as these might be to define architecture, or put limits on an ever changing, transforming, and expanding discipline. This may prove an impossible endeavor but, through studying sketches, a better understanding of their role emerges, thus proposing a better understanding of architecture itself.

Architectural sketches, like the process of architecture, reflect the past, facilitate the present and attempt to foretell the future. Their meaning remains personal and speaks to each individual architect. As with memory, imagination, fantasy and play, it is possible to examine their traits, but as entities they may remain elusive. This elusive quality exhibits strength not a weakness. As the term *elusive* refers to the concept of play, these playful allusions facilitate the ability to view more of sketches' meaning.

The inability to adequately define what sketches mean to each and every architect compels a speculation about their thoughts. With the conjecture concerning the nature of *likeness*, concepts of imitation, copy, replica, similarity, resemblance, analogy, metaphor and allusion all have overlapping meanings. Each removes a dimension in abstraction. Not merely modes of imitation, various writers on aesthetics have assigned specific meaning to these words. Their meaning depends upon a relationship to an intentional concept. Visual likeness allows sketches to function for architects as communicative, imaginative, remembrance, discoveries and thinking devices.

Some contemporary definitions of words like imitation, copy and replica treat the object and its representation as almost identical in all dimensions. The Greek's phrase for 'fine arts' was 'imitative arts' (Aristotle, 1951). In literature the term's use began with Plato, and was probably common in usage to distinguish between fine art and industrial production (Aristotle, 1951). In contrast to Plato's notion of the real world as mere imitation, Aristotle held that: '… the artist may "imitate things as they ought to be"' (Aristotle, 1951: 122). He used imitation to show another dimension of reality. 'A work of art is a likeness or reproduction of an original, and not a symbolic representation of it' (Aristotle, 1951: 124). His words impart the view of an imitation, not necessarily as an identical image but as an alteration of the original.

Umberto Eco writes that the images need only be similar to an original in order for their creator to gain knowledge and communicate ideas. 'A transformation does not suggest the idea of natural correspondence; it is rather the consequence of rules and artifice ... Similitude is *produced* and must be learned' (Eco, 1979: 200). Architects learn to view one thing as another, and thus make individual examples of similitude.

Although they are close in meaning, Michel Foucault finds a difference between 'similitude' and 'resemblance':

Resemblance has a 'model', an original element that orders and hierarchizes the increasingly less faithful copies that can be struck from it. Resemblance presupposes a primary reference that prescribes and classes. The similar develops in series that have neither beginning nor end, that can be followed in one direction as easily as in another, that obey no hierarchy, but propagate themselves from small differences among small differences. Resemblance serves representation, which rules over it; similitude serves repetition, which ranges across it. Resemblance predicates itself upon a model it must return to and reveal; similitude circulates the simulacrum as an indefinite a reversible relation of the similar to the similar. (Foucault, 1982: 44)

From this statement it would seem that caricature is more accurately described in terms of resemblance than similitude. Foucault's words suggest the tautological aspects of similitude. Sketches act as metaphors because of their substitution (transference) qualities (Gombrich, 1963). A metaphor implies a reference and, likewise, both art and sketching refer to something beyond (Gombrich, 1963). It takes the associative qualities of imagination to bridge metaphorical meanings. D.G. James discusses metaphor in his article on metaphor and symbol:

Now metaphor, ... is one of the forms of symbol: it is the imagination of one thing in the form of another; it is the mode in which the nature, the being, the imagined extra-sensual essence of a thing, is represented by the identification with the apparently different; and it is a procedure for which science can give no warrant; the scientific use of language must abhor metaphor. But metaphor is the nerve or heart of all poetic creation. But still, metaphor is only the way in which the imagination works; it never adds up to a statement and doctrine. (James, 1960: 100)

In allusion, there is even less *likeness* between a substitute and the original than with metaphor. Sketches act as substitutes in *likeness* for a mental impression in the imagination. Standing for something else, the sketch is not a symbol but resides metaphorically in place of something else. Umberto Eco's concepts of strong and weak codes are relevant here.

The universe of visual communications reminds us that we communicate both on the basis of strong codes (such as language) and indeed very strong ones (such as the Morse Code) and on the basis of weak codes, which are barely defined and continuously changing, and in which the free variants prevail over the pertinent features. (Eco, 1979: 214)

Sketches epitomize a 'weak code'; and thus they compare to allusion and metaphor. The treatment of minimal likeness is reminiscent of analogy or allegory. The word *analogy* comes from the Greek meaning equality in ratio or proportion. Its definition ranges from the equivalence or *likeness* of relations and resemblance of things with regard to some circumstances, or effects, to similarity (Oxford English Dictionary). The relative *likeness* may determine the comparison between two things.

An allegory approaches a metaphor in that it is a figurative treatment of one subject under the guise of another, but allegory still depends on a comparison in terms of ratio or proportion. Similarly,

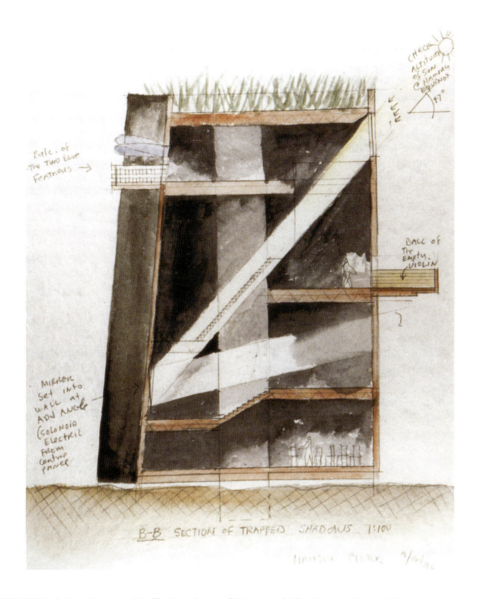

FIGURE 6.1   Steven Holl; Section of Trapped Shadows, Knut Hamsun project.

sketches might hold some proportional qualities in comparison to the original, but the issue here lies in the nature of the original. Jean Baudrillard questions the image as real, or more than real, when he discusses the perception and interpretation of media. 'For us the medium, the image medium, has imposed itself between the real and the imaginary, upsetting the balance between the two, with a kind of a fatality which has it own logic' (1987: 30). With this in mind, sketches hover between the two and possibly cannot be declared as either. Since sketches in architecture can be used in many ways and take many forms, it is clearly the quality of *likeness* which unites them.

This beautifully articulated section for the Knut Hamsun project by Steven Holl (Figure 6.1) tells a story of relative *likeness*. The watercolor sketch is entitled *Section of Trapped Shadows*. Black watercolor enhances the stark white stream of light emitting from an opening in the wall on the top right corner of the building. This profile exhibits the relative proportion and placement of floors, walls, and balconies. The column of light has been calculated to flow into the space at a specific angle and thus at a specific time of day. The space has been given scale with stairs, figures, and some furniture. It appears Holl was attempting to visualize the space with this provocative band of illumination to break diagonally through the different levels. Most likely, it was important for him to attain a sense of 'reality' but also control the light in a conceptual way.

Although the volume in the completed building may not appear exactly like the section sketch, it conveys a conceptual intention. Here, the desire seems to be a distinctive stream of light, so defined that it assumes volumetric qualities. Holl would know that the light would disperse and reflect to achieve a softer more modeled effect when constructed, but it was important to demonstrate the angles and the intended outcome.

This sketch cannot replicate the exact atmosphere of the space, but it could assist to understand the relationships, anticipate the sun angles, and simulate the conceptual intention. This exaggeration shows the purpose and also describes the way the illumination would act. As a diagram it provided sufficient *likeness* to understand the spatial relationships and the effect of the wall opening. The sketch may have confirmed, for Holl, a competent resemblance for reference.

In his book *Blink*, Malcolm Gladwell writes about how unexplainable connections in our brains present association of *likeness* and recognition. When describing the way our perceptions draw conclusions and make instantaneous comparisons, he uses the example of bird watchers' ability to immediately recognize various species of birds:

> *Most of bird identification is based on a sort of subjective impression – the way a bird moves and little instantaneous appearances at different angles and sequences of different appearances, and as it turns its head and as it flies and as it turns around, you see sequences of different shapes and angles, … all that combines to create a unique impression of a bird that can't really be taken apart and described in words. When it comes down to being in the field and looking at a bird, you don't take the time to analyze it and say it shows this, this, and this; therefore it must be this species. It's more natural and instinctive. After a lot of practice, you look at the bird, and it triggers little switches in your brain. It looks right. You know what it is at a glance. (Gladwell, 2005: 44–45)*

This occurrence usually emanates from experience helping observers recognize *likeness*. Gladwell also suggests that much of this recognition and adjustment, or quick unexplainable connections, is subconscious and touches upon body memory. This readjustment and refinement take on qualities of second nature. Gladwell relates a story of exceptional tennis players about their success. Tennis Pro coach Vic Braden queries tennis players ' …about why and how they play the way they do', and invariably he comes away disappointed, '…they do things they cannot explain or are not conscious of' (Gladwell, 2005: 67–68). They make conscious and also these subconscious corrections in their play to refine and improve performance. Likewise architects, using their judgment, continually perfect their sketches to meet conceptual notions or to 'make and match' an impression in their mind's eye. This mental impression as compared to the sketched image is a constant refinement of *likeness*.

Not all architects draw from imagination, but instead may start by drawing a shape or form and then use that image to summon new images. Often they doodle when conversing with a client. Whatever personal method they use for inspiration or association, these sketches convey some elements of communication.

Promoting the special talents of architects becomes advantageous. Architects sell a service often viewed by laymen as exceptional, if not magical. Historically, artists were reported to be able to make 'things' come to life. Daedalus, in mythical stories, made statues so lifelike they ' …had to be fastened down, to prevent them from walking away' (Kris and Kurz, 1979: 68–68). This myth of artists/architects in control of images infiltrates our society. Eco explains that anyone with an ability to draw is set apart as having a special secret or knowing another language:

> *This also helps us to understand why a person who speaks does not seem to be born with any special ability, but if someone can draw, he already seems 'different' from others, because we recognize in him*

the ability to articulate elements of a code which does not belong to the whole group; and we recognize in him an autonomy in relation to normal systems which we do not recognize in any speaker except a poet (Eco, 1979: 215).

The ability to conceive and produce images sets architects apart from members of non-artistic professions. The skill to communicate with drawings preserves this separation. The power to relate to an original, to what is depicted, further expresses a capacity to assimilate *likeness*. Kris and Kurz, in a book on legends and myths of artists, write that there is potency in control of the image, especially when that image holds the soul of that substance:

Here we come upon the most common practice associated with the equation of picture and depicted, namely, the belief in magic, especially effigy magic – the belief that 'a man's soul resides in his image, that those who possess this image also hold power over that person, and that all the pain inflicted on the image must be felt by the person it represents'. (Kris and Kurz, 1979: 73)

Obviously the building is not a person, but if architects can be compared to thaumaturgists, then the image has a 'life' that evokes fear of alteration. In some way, architects do assign drawings anthropomorphic qualities and, to obliterate them, may destroy their life and the life of the building in a metaphoric manner. This study has viewed caricature as a system that distorts and transforms images, an activity that could not have taken place before the time of the Renaissance. The power to deform recognizes a control over an architectural environment, and presents the faculty for judgment and evaluation. Architects have had the capacity to distort and change images, but the pertinent issue remains the ability of architects to manipulate *likeness*.

DIGITAL SKETCHES

Architects, architectural educators, and students have recently been utilizing digital means to question *likeness* and expand upon definitions of sketches as 'outlines', or as 'preliminary or preparatory' to something else. If a sketch has temporal qualities, then it is possible to ask whether digital manipulations can be considered sketches. Once used primarily for presentation renderings and construction documents, drawings constructed digitally contain several elements that could unite them under the label of 'sketches'.

Many programs for the computer allow quick manipulation of form. This software encourages the basic shapes of a future building to be constructed in a few minutes. The fact that these digital musings are in a machine, and easily changed, means that their comparison to sketches becomes more evident. In most cases, these applications permit simple form generation that can be refined and reworked at a later time. The fact that they procreate with a click of the hand means they do not require the pondering of a rendering. The ability to 'pull' a corner of a plane into a three-dimensional form makes building solids easy, but this process often limits the images on the screen to be simple platonic shapes. Thus, these simple forms may replicate the sketches' characteristic of being an 'outline'. In most cases, these simple forms, often wire frame, are the beginnings for further manipulation and elaboration causing them to act as preliminary to a completed design. They also do not need to, at this early stage, replicate the completed building in its entirety. The loose and irresponsible connections that defy gravity or construction conventions are sufficient for conceptualization. Their beauty lies in their ability to be easily deformed and dissected.

This digital image (Figure 6.2) demonstrates qualities of a sketch. Mark Foster Gage and Marc Clemenceau Bailly opened their firm Gage/Clemenceau Architects in 2002. Based in New York City, their work has included residential renovations, small buildings, and competitions. They are

FIGURE 6.2   Mark Foster Gage; Wallpaper.

both educators and see their office as a laboratory of investigation. The philosophy of their practice embraces continual experimentation with shapes and new technologies.

This study, entitled *Wallpaper*, is a preliminary sketch for a library addition in Stockholm, Sweden. These architects were exploring a series of floor plates resembling leaves on a stalk, cantilevered, and unlike traditional stacked floors. The petal-like floors appear organic, with light oval extensions. The translucency of the technique adds to their airy lightness. The construction of the shapes gives them dimension rather than resembling floors. For Gage and Bailly, these images suggest a conceptual beginning with more affinity to a sketch than a floor plan. Experimenting with overlapping form does not question the connections or construction techniques but instead presents provocative suggestions about the future of architectural shape. As a preliminary rendering for the library addition in Stockholm, the leaves and stalks now take three-dimensional form. Strewn across the page, the shapes are devoid of context and suggest many possibilities to their makers.

A second sketch from Gage/Clemenceau Architects (Figure 6.3) appears to propose an architectural space. Called the *VERY LARGE INTERIOR apocalypse*, this white shiny future-esque space considers scale and structure. The fluid forms wind and flow resembling molded plastic. Using digital means to explore the potentialities of new materials, this sketch evokes a future at the same time as it defines a plausible construction. The computer, with little concern for gravity and structural integrity, may subscribe to a strategy rather than a reality. The open form defines spaces that drift into a darkened background. Gage implies that this perspective is a quick sketch to visualize the quality of the interior space. It evokes more emotion and associative imagination than information about enclosure.

In another example from Gage/Clemenceau Architects, Figure 6.4 describes the open-ended qualities that make some of these digital images comparable to sketches. Once formed, allusions and associations can suggest various functions to the architects who create them. Designers often draw abstractly hoping to receive inspiration, or direction, from the images that emerge from the

FIGURE 6.3   Mark Foster Gage; VERY LARGE INTERIOR apocalypse.

FIGURE 6.4   Mark Foster Gage; Final Blue copy.

process. The fear of the blank page may originate from the lack of stimulation, because boundaries create opportunities for judgment and critique.

Gage writes about how the process of review changed the purpose of the sketch: '[t]his one was actually a digitally scripted study in form. It was originally going to be a library in the Czech

Republic but didn't really work the way we wanted it to. So then "surface" magazine wanted it and turned it into a desktop organizer.'[1] If a sketch is the medium to facilitate a process then this digital image is functioning as a sketch. It 'speaks' to the architects in a dialogue that decides its appropriateness. When viewing some of the digital musings by architects, the images may appear distinctly personal, but the fact that not everyone can perceive the information they hold does not diminish their value. This is the manner of sketches and, similarly, hand sketches may not be useable, or decipherable, by anyone except their author.

LIKENESS AND THE MARGINAL

When architects operate sketches they primarily perform as personal dialogue. Because sketches embody knowledge and belief they need not present a 'perfect' *likeness*. Architects believe in their sketches and how they communicate. Thus, the sketch may be abstracted or fragmented, but still provide a useful forum for exchange. This suggests a theory that abstracted sketches may be uniquely viewed by architects. Possibly, each image takes on a 'life of its own', or becomes metaphysical as it reveals information only to the author. Kris and Kurz suggest magical belief by artists allowing an image to be removed from 'realistic' representation. They write: '… the "stronger" the belief in the magic function of the image, in the identity of picture and depicted, the less important the nature of that image' (Kris and Kurz, 1979: 77).

Most architects would find it difficult to state that they believe their sketches to be 'magical'. However, it may be easy for them to admit that sketches are often enchanting and provide unexpected results. The surprises might stem from a vague image that provides new ideas in association. Again, this study has returned to the key notion of *likeness*, and the role of resemblance:

> *… whenever a high degree of magic power is attributed to an object … its resemblance to nature is rarely of decisive importance … the closer the symbol (picture) stands to what is symbolized (depicted), the less is the outward resemblance: the further apart, the greater is the resemblance. (Kris and Kurz, 1979: 77–78)*

Kris and Kurz offer an example of a myth from art history, in which an artist, when drawing the eyes on a dragon, found that the dragon flew away. They suggest from this myth that the artist who does not draw the eyes of a subject can '… prevent it from coming wholly to life' (1979: 83). This example also suggests the power of the artist over the image created. This concept recalls the previous architectural examples that avoided depicting a context. Stopping short of complete illusion possibly sustains the enchanting qualities of the image. Architects may avoid 'eyes' to keep the drawing from approaching the practical and definite. Its 'concreteness' does not allow for change, or the metaphor's dependent on *likeness*. The abstract image may become magical in its ability to play with imagination and support dialogue.

To reiterate, the words used to describe *likeness* are numerous; each assesses a slightly different meaning. The unifying feature is that of visual resemblance in imagery. Sketches furnish a mode for dialogue and communicating in the seeing world of architecture. A quote by D.G. James brings to light some of the intangible qualities of *likeness* for architectural sketches:

> *… what lies beyond the strictly observable, measurable and verifiable aspects of things? … what are 'things in themselves'? … [b]rought thus sharply to the boundaries of demonstrable, i.e. scientific,*

---

[1] When asked to provide some background on the digital sketches, Mark Foster Gage wrote to me about how they use these images in their office.

knowledge of the world, we are confronted by the illimitable, unplumbed world lying beyond the narrow scope of the discourse of science and the understandable, and in the face of this meta-sensual world, the world as it is in itself, the unknown being of things, we are left to wonder and surmise; it is from this wonder and surmise that philosophy and art alike take their origin: and it is at this point that metaphor and symbol come into operation. (James, 1960: 98)

Sketches evoke qualities of the marginal in that they are vague and intangible. Although most architects constantly utilize sketches, these sketches reside on the boundaries of things tangible, as they contain endless possibilities. Their vagueness invites projection, association, and interpretation. These qualities suggest their vacillation between things known and those that are unknown. As transitory elements they move easily between a text and its boundaries.

A definition of marginal implies an area that is part of a surface which lies immediately within its boundary, especially when in some way marked off or distinguished from the rest of the surface. A margin describes a condition that closely approximates to the limit below or beyond which something ceases to be possible or desirable. It accounts for unseen contingencies, and inhabits the edge of a text, often used for summary or commentary. Sketches may be compared to a marginal position in their incompleteness. They hover on the edge between being something and being unintelligible. Sketches with this vagueness might not have a clear objective or a clear interpretation.

Similar to play, which defies clearly defined boundaries, they may coincide with haphazard action. The marginal summons that which hovers on the edge, both literally and figuratively. This position connotes danger, revolution, pure possibility, fantasy, and irresponsibility. The concept of the marginal also suggests the doubtful, the unknown, and fearful living. 'Living on the edge' is distinctly living in a state of the unknown, not within the lines of accepted behavior; it contains an element of risk. The edge may speak of *likeness* to an original, a tentative connection, and this connection may require knowledge of an intention to be comprehended. Sketches' irresponsibility exhibits their affinity for the poetic and ephemeral.

Historically, the margins of a book or manuscript present opportunities for notes or commentary. These edges may contain decorative illuminations or humorous visual arabesques meant especially for diversion. They have become comic relief for a serious and important document. Margins are abstract and pull away from the main text, possibly similar to being outside oneself. The margins in a book represent the tolerance for binding. They are the play when printing, so that the text is contained on a page. Similarly, with sketches, the image exists close to the border between reality and unreality. They might differ from the whole, but affect the placement and boundaries of the whole. A border graphically makes a text appealing, supporting and composing the framework within which the text may be read. An argument, dialectic, communication or conversation may act similarly. Without the uncertainty the dialogue is unnecessary.

The following two projects (Figures 6.5 and 6.6), from the realm of academia, reveal digital and analog hybrid explorations into the creative process. Professors Julio Bermudez of the University of Utah, Bennett Neiman of Texas Tech University, and Tim Castillo at the University the New Mexico challenge their students to combine various media to experiment with the '... interface between analog and digital systems of architectural making and thinking.'[2]

The students use photography, hand sketching, scanned objects, analog model construction, and digital modeling to design spatial allusions. These hybrid sketches present space and form with intention but without conventional building programs. The projects can be labeled sketches as they lack qualities that translate into buildings. The images evoke a future architecture, but do not prescribe definitions for construction. They are fanciful and expressive alluding to conceptual notions

---

[2] From studio materials and conference papers by Julio Bermudez and Bennett Neiman.

FIGURE 6.5   Julio Bermudez, Bennett Neiman, Tim Castillo; Digital Analog Studio.

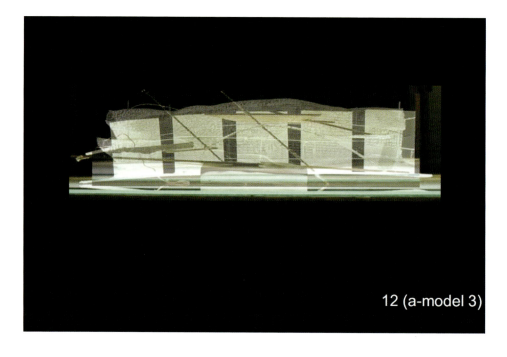

FIGURE 6.6   Julio Bermudez, Bennett Neiman, Tim Castillo; Digital Analog Studio.

of architecture. Through techniques of scanning, manipulation, and deformation they are constantly in flux and thrive on the indeterminate. Each of these images projects possibilities, and thus they act as sketches in the manner of something preliminary and preparatory to further development.

Cryptic and interpretable, architects must be able to comprehend and learn from the marks made. They project onto a sketch in anticipation of a building. In an attempt to visualize the unknown a sketch is a preparation, a fragment of the finished entity. As marginal, sketches provide for the unseen contingencies, because they account for poetic and emotional reflection not always found in representative media. Architectural sketches are easily changed and can utilize various combinations to facilitate dialogue. Sketches are active, as the mind can play with and ponder them long after the initial action is completed. They identify with the conceptual and that which is more discernable. Undetermined, they extend between two realms and, like the grotesque, act as intermediaries in the design process. They have few rules or boundaries, beyond those imposed by the architect's imagination.

CONCLUSION

To conclude, it is important to reiterate how vital architectural sketches are to architects, and to the design process, in their facilitation of visual dialogue. They embody a polemical dimension which begins to elucidate complex concepts. They encourage the potential to envision the future, which promotes decision-making. Being abstract and incomplete, architectural sketches support the projection of thoughts and facilitate evaluation. The ability to critique enhances judgment, and these sketches are the medium for that activity.

Again, architectural sketches are the instruments for a design dialogue. In seeking to understand them through faculties of the mind, memory, imagination and fantasy, the philosophical aspects of play, and the literary and aesthetic characteristics of caricature and the grotesque, this study moves toward comprehension of how architects think, communicate and design. Architectural sketches sustain the dialogue which assist architects to make architecture.

BIBLIOGRAPHY

(1971). *The Compact Edition of the Oxford English Dictionary*. Oxford University Press.
Aristotle. (1951). *Aristotle's Theory of Poetry and Fine Art*. Dover.
Baudrillard, J. (1983). *Simulations*. Semiotext.
Baudrillard, J. (1987). *The Evil Demon of Images*. Left Bank Books.
Baudrillard, J. (1988). *The Ecstasy of Communication*. Semiotext.
Benjamin, W. (1968). *Illuminations*. Schocken Books.
Collingwood, R.G. (1964). *The Principles of Art*. Oxford University Press.
Croce, B. (1970). *Aesthetic*. MacMillan.
Eco, U. (1979). *A Theory of Semiotics*. Indiana University Press.
Foucault, M. (1982). *This is not a Pipe*. University of California Press.
Gaut, B.N. and Lopes, D. (2005). *The Routledge Companion to Aesthetics*. Routledge.
Gladwell, M. (2005). *Blink*. Little Brown.
Goldie, P. and Schellekens, E. (2007). *Philosophy and Conceptual Art*. Oxford University Press.
Gombrich, E.H. (1963). *Meditations on a Hobby Horse*. University of Chicago Press.
Hutcheon, L. (1985). *A Theory of Parody; the Teachings of Twentieth-Century Art Forms*. Methuen.
James, D.G. (1960). *Metaphor and Symbol*. Butterworth's Scientific Publications.

Kris, E. and Kurz, O. (1979). *Legend, Myth, and Magic in the Image of the Artist*. Yale University Press.

Levinson, J. (2006). *Contemplating Art; Essays in Aesthetics*. Oxford University Press.

Moholy-Nagy, L. (1947). *Vision in Motion*. Cuneo Press.

Steenbergen, C., Mihl, H., Rehm, W. and Aerts, F. (2002). *Architectural Design and Composition*. Thoth.

Wollheim, R. (1966). *Art and Its objects*. Harper and Row.

INDEX

DATE DUE